A GIFT FOR:

_____

Blessed is the man who trusts in the LORD,
    whose confidence is in him.

Jeremiah 17:7

FROM:

_____

Promises for Life for Men
Copyright © 2006 by the Zondervan Corporation

Requests for information should be addressed to:

Zondervan, *Grand Rapids, Michigan* 49530

ISBN-10: 0-310-81585-1
ISBN-13: 978-0-310-81585-3

Excerpts taken from: *The New Men's Devotional Bible, New International Version*, copyright © 2006 by the Zondervan Corporation.

All Scripture quotations, unless otherwise indicated, are taken from the *Holy Bible: New International Version*®. NIV®. Copyright © 1973, 1978, 1984 by International Bible Society. Used by permission of Zondervan. All rights reserved.

Interior design by Mark Veldheer

Printed in China

11 12 • 7 6

promises FOR LIFE FOR
men

new international version

ZONDERVAN®

contents
promises for life on

Adversity 6
Anxiety 12
Choices 18
Commitment 24
Compassion 30
Contentment 36
Courage 42
Eternal Life 48
Faithfulness 54
Forgiveness 60
Friends 64
Giftedness 68
Gratitude 72
Grief 78
Hope 84
Humility 90
Identity 94
Individualism 100
Integrity 106
Leadership 110

Listening. 116
Love 120
Mentors 126
Money 128
Obedience 134
Possessions 136
Prayer. 138
Purpose. 144
Righteous Living 148
Security 152
Serving. 158
Spiritual Growth 162
Strength 168
Suffering. 172
Temptation 178
Trust. 182
Unity 186
Wisdom 190
Work. 196
Worship 200

promises for life
on adversity

If God is for us, who can be against us?

Romans 8:31

"Because he loves me," says the LORD, "I will
          rescue him;
    I will protect him, for he acknowledges
          my name.
He will call upon me, and I will answer him;
    I will be with him in trouble,
    I will deliver him and honor him."

Psalm 91:14–15

*Thanks be to God! He gives us the victory through
our Lord Jesus Christ.*

1 Corinthians 15:57

*Jesus said, "I tell you the truth, if you have faith
as small as a mustard seed, you can say to this
mountain, 'Move from here to there' and it will move.
Nothing will be impossible for you."*

Matthew 17:20

*Jesus said, "In this world you will have trouble. But
take heart! I have overcome the world."*

John 16:33

We are more than conquerors through him who loved us. For I am convinced that neither death nor life, neither angels nor demons, neither the present nor the future, nor any powers, neither height nor depth, nor anything else in all creation, will be able to separate us from the love of God that is in Christ Jesus our Lord.

Romans 8:37–39

Is any one of you in trouble? He should pray.

James 5:13

With your help I can advance against a troop;
    with my God I can scale a wall.

Psalm 18:29

Let us not become weary in doing good, for at the proper time we will reap a harvest if we do not give up.

Galatians 6:9

God is our refuge and strength,
    an ever-present help in trouble.

Psalm 46:1

promises for life
on adversity

When the servant of [Elisha] got up and went out early the next morning, an army with horses and chariots had surrounded the city. "Oh, my lord, what shall we do?" the servant asked. "Don't be afraid," the prophet answered. "Those who are with us are more than those who are with them." And Elisha prayed, "O LORD, open his eyes so he may see." Then the LORD opened the servant's eyes, and he looked and saw the hills full of horses and chariots of fire all around Elisha.

2 Kings 6:15–17

God has said,
"Never will I leave you;
    never will I forsake you."
So we say with confidence,
"The Lord is my helper; I will not be afraid."

Hebrews 13:5–6

The one who is in you is greater than the one who is in the world.

1 John 4:4

Stand firm and you will see the deliverance the Lord will bring you today.

Exodus 14:13

As servants of God we commend ourselves in every way: in great endurance; in troubles, hardships and distresses; in beatings, imprisonments and riots; in hard work, sleepless nights and hunger; in purity, understanding, patience and kindness; in the Holy Spirit and in sincere love; in truthful speech and in the power of God; with weapons of righteousness in the right hand and in the left.

2 Corinthians 6:4–7

Thanks be to God, who always leads us in triumphal procession in Christ and through us spreads everywhere the fragrance of the knowledge of him.

2 Corinthians 2:14

A righteous man may have many troubles,
   but the Lord delivers him from them all.

Psalm 34:19

for men

Jesus said, "With God all things are possible."

Matthew 19:26

Put on the full armor of God, so that when the day of evil comes, you may be able to stand your ground, and after you have done everything, to stand. Stand firm then, with the belt of truth buckled around your waist, with the breastplate of righteousness in place, and with your feet fitted with the readiness that comes from the gospel of peace. In addition to all this, take up the shield of faith, with which you can extinguish all the flaming arrows of the evil one. Take the helmet of salvation and the sword of the Spirit, which is the word of God. And pray in the Spirit on all occasions with all kinds of prayers and requests.

Ephesians 6:13–18

Our light and momentary troubles are achieving for us an eternal glory that far outweighs them all.

2 Corinthians 4:17

devotional thought
on adversity

Caleb faced pressure to despair after his spy mission in Canaan. Ten of his fellow spies panicked when they saw the size of the people living in Canaan—the enemies the Israelites would need to defeat in order to claim the promised land. "There's no way we can beat them," the other spies reported. "They're too powerful."

Caleb's scouting report reflected a different perspective. He wasn't impressed by the size of the Anakites—he was bowled over by the power of the One who held back the waters of the Red Sea. He didn't fear the fighting force of the Amalekites—it paled in comparison with the artillery of the One who brought Egypt to its knees.

Caleb surveyed the obstacles in front of him and concluded that nothing was a match for God's power.

Have you reached the same conclusion regarding the obstacles in your life?

promises for life
on anxiety

Jesus said, "Do not worry about your life, what you will eat or drink; or about your body, what you will wear. Is not life more important than food, and the body more important than clothes? Look at the birds of the air; they do not sow or reap or store away in barns, and yet your heavenly Father feeds them. Are you not much more valuable than they?"

Matthew 6:25–26

You will keep in perfect peace
> him whose mind is steadfast,
> because he trusts in you.

Isaiah 26:3

Do not be anxious about anything, but in everything, by prayer and petition, with thanksgiving, present your requests to God. And the peace of God, which transcends all understanding, will guard your hearts and your minds in Christ Jesus.

Philippians 4:6–7

Jesus said, "See how the lilies of the field grow. They do not labor or spin. Yet I tell you that not even Solomon in all his splendor was dressed like one of these. If that is how God clothes the grass of the field, which is here today and tomorrow is thrown into the fire, will he not much more clothe you?"

Matthew 6:28–30

Trust in the LORD with all your heart
    and lean not on your own understanding;
in all your ways acknowledge him,
    and he will make your paths straight.

Proverbs 3:5–6

He who dwells in the shelter of the Most High
    will rest in the shadow of the Almighty.
I will say of the LORD, "He is my refuge and
        my fortress,
    my God, in whom I trust."

Psalm 91:1–2

promises for life
on anxiety

*Jesus said, "Do not worry, saying, 'What shall we eat?'
or 'What shall we drink?' or 'What shall we wear?'
For the pagans run after all these things, and your
heavenly Father knows that you need them. But seek
first his kingdom and his righteousness, and all these
things will be given to you as well."*

Matthew 6:31–33

The LORD bless you
  and keep you;
the LORD make his face shine upon you
  and be gracious to you;
the LORD turn his face toward you
  and give you peace.

Numbers 6:24–26

*The apostle Paul wrote, "Whatever is true, whatever
is noble, whatever is right, whatever is pure, whatever
is lovely, whatever is admirable—if anything is
excellent or praiseworthy—think about such things.
Whatever you have learned or received or heard from
me, or seen in me—put it into practice. And the God
of peace will be with you."*

Philippians 4:8–9

Jesus said, "Do not worry about tomorrow, for tomorrow will worry about itself."

Matthew 6:34

The LORD watches over you—
    the LORD is your shade at your right hand;
the sun will not harm you by day,
    nor the moon by night.
The LORD will keep you from all harm—
    he will watch over your life;
the LORD will watch over your coming and going
    both now and forevermore.

Psalm 121:5–8

Jesus said, "Do not let your hearts be troubled. Trust in God; trust also in me."

John 14:1

When I am afraid,
    I will trust in you.
In God, whose word I praise,
    in God I trust; I will not be afraid.

Psalm 56:3–4

for men

Jesus said, "Who of you by worrying can add a single hour to his life?"

Matthew 6:27

The LORD is my shepherd, I shall not be in want.
 He makes me lie down in green pastures,
he leads me beside quiet waters,
 he restores my soul.
He guides me in paths of righteousness
 for his name's sake.
Even though I walk
 through the valley of the shadow of death,
I will fear no evil,
 for you are with me;
your rod and your staff,
 they comfort me.

Psalm 23:1–4

Jesus said, "Are not two sparrows sold for a penny? Yet not one of them will fall to the ground apart from the will of your Father. And even the very hairs of your head are all numbered. So don't be afraid; you are worth more than many sparrows."

Matthew 10:29–31

devotional thought
on anxiety

Being the fickle human beings we are, sometimes we have an "out of sight, out of mind" mentality when it comes to God's blessings. Despite experiencing prior blessings from God, the trouble of the moment is all we see. So we look for comfort in the first fast fix we can find.

When the going gets unpleasant, instead of toughing it out and seeking God for strength and insight, it's all too easy to create an escape. Maybe it's a hunting trip, an outing to a football game, or taking the whole family to dinner and a movie—anything other than facing a tough issue with prayer and patience.

So what should you do? Rather than seeking the idols of pleasure—escape and comfort—simply seek the blessings of your relationship with God.

promises for life
on choices

Your word, O LORD, is a lamp to my feet
　　and a light for my path.

Psalm 119:105

*Whether you turn to the right or to the left, your ears
will hear a voice behind you, saying, "This is the way;
walk in it."*

Isaiah 30:21

Show me your ways, O LORD,
　　teach me your paths;
guide me in your truth and teach me,
　　for you are God my Savior,
　　and my hope is in you all day long.

Psalm 25:4–5

*If you do what is right, will you not be accepted?
But if you do not do what is right, sin is crouching
at your door.*

Genesis 4:7

[The LORD] guides me in paths of righteousness
　　for his name's sake.

Psalm 23:3

Be very careful, then, how you live—not as unwise but as wise, making the most of every opportunity, because the days are evil. Therefore do not be foolish, but understand what the Lord's will is.

Ephesians 5:15–17

If any of you lacks wisdom, he should ask God, who gives generously to all without finding fault, and it will be given to him.

James 1:5

Good and upright is the LORD;
    therefore he instructs sinners in his ways.
He guides the humble in what is right
    and teaches them his way.

Psalm 25:8–9

Do what is right and good in the LORD's sight, so that it may go well with you.

Deuteronomy 6:18

Let the wise listen and add to their learning,
    and let the discerning get guidance.

Proverbs 1:5

promises for life
on choices

You were once darkness, but now you are light in the Lord. Live as children of light (for the fruit of the light consists in all goodness, righteousness and truth) and find out what pleases the Lord. Have nothing to do with the fruitless deeds of darkness.

Ephesians 5:8–11

My son, keep your father's commands
    and do not forsake your mother's teaching.
Bind them upon your heart forever;
    fasten them around your neck.
When you walk, they will guide you;
    when you sleep, they will watch over you;
    when you awake, they will speak to you.
For these commands are a lamp,
    this teaching is a light,
and the corrections of discipline
    are the way to life.

Proverbs 6:20–23

Let us put aside the deeds of darkness and put on the armor of light.

Romans 13:12

Jesus said, "Enter through the narrow gate. For wide is the gate and broad is the road that leads to destruction, and many enter through it. But small is the gate and narrow the road that leads to life, and only a few find it."

Matthew 7:13–14

The path of the righteous is like the first gleam
of dawn,
    shining ever brighter till the full light of day.

Proverbs 4:18

Be careful to do what the LORD your God has commanded you; do not turn aside to the right or to the left. Walk in all the way that the LORD your God has commanded you, so that you may live and prosper and prolong your days in the land that you will possess.

Deuteronomy 5:32–33

God is our God for ever and ever;
    he will be our guide even to the end.

Psalm 48:14

for men

Live a life worthy of the calling you have received.

Ephesians 4:1

The LORD gives wisdom,
and from his mouth come knowledge
and understanding.
He holds victory in store for the upright,
he is a shield to those whose walk is blameless,
for he guards the course of the just
and protects the way of his faithful ones.

Proverbs 2:6–8

Just as he who called you is holy, so be holy in all you do; for it is written: "Be holy, because I am holy."

1 Peter 1:15–16

I have set before you life and death, blessings and curses. Now choose life, so that you and your children may live and that you may love the LORD your God, listen to his voice, and hold fast to him.

Deuteronomy 30:19–20

devotional thought
on choices

God always instructs his people first with his words. Then, if they don't listen, he lets them touch the stove and get burned. Jeremiah hoped that the people of Judah would listen. Instead, they touched the stove of rebellion, refused to listen to Jeremiah's words, and the Babylonians mastered them.

Sadly, many of us are like the people of Judah in this story—we're slow to listen by faith and respond with obedience, and we stubbornly plow ahead with our own agenda until the heat rises and we find ourselves in trouble.

God wants only the best for his children. But the reality is that we're faced with choices every day that determine the circumstances in which we find ourselves. If we take the time to prayerfully consider the decisions we face, we have a better chance of making the right choices for ourselves and our families.

"You will seek me and find me when you seek me with all your heart," declares the LORD.

Jeremiah 29:13

Love the LORD your God with all your heart and with all your soul and with all your strength.

Deuteronomy 6:5

Commit your way to the LORD;
  trust in him and he will do this:
He will make your righteousness shine like the dawn,
  the justice of your cause like the noonday sun.

Psalm 37:5–6

Jesus said, "The kingdom of heaven is like a merchant looking for fine pearls. When he found one of great value, he went away and sold everything he had and bought it."

Matthew 13:45–46

Stand firm. Let nothing move you. Always give yourselves fully to the work of the Lord, because you know that your labor in the Lord is not in vain.

1 Corinthians 15:58

for men

Your hearts must be fully committed to the LORD our God, to live by his decrees and obey his commands.

1 Kings 8:61

When the kindness and love of God our Savior appeared, he saved us, not because of righteous things we had done, but because of his mercy. He saved us through the washing of rebirth and renewal by the Holy Spirit, whom he poured out on us generously through Jesus Christ our Savior, so that, having been justified by his grace, we might become heirs having the hope of eternal life. This is a trustworthy saying. And I want you to stress these things, so that those who have trusted in God may be careful to devote themselves to doing what is good.

Titus 3:4–8

Commit to the LORD whatever you do,
    and your plans will succeed.

Proverbs 16:3

promises for life
on commitment

Jesus went out and saw a tax collector by the name of Levi sitting at his tax booth. "Follow me," Jesus said to him, and Levi got up, left everything and followed him.

Luke 5:27–28

Be devoted to one another in brotherly love. Honor one another above yourselves. Never be lacking in zeal, but keep your spiritual fervor, serving the Lord. Be joyful in hope, patient in affliction, faithful in prayer.

Romans 12:10–12

Let us not become weary in doing good, for at the proper time we will reap a harvest if we do not give up. Therefore, as we have opportunity, let us do good to all people, especially to those who belong to the family of believers.

Galatians 6:9–10

Jesus said, "Everyone who has left houses or brothers
or sisters or father or mother or children or fields for
my sake will receive a hundred times as much and will
inherit eternal life."

Matthew 19:29

Put on the full armor of God, so that when the day of
evil comes, you may be able to stand your ground, and
after you have done everything, to stand.

Ephesians 6:13

Hezekiah did … what was good and right and
faithful before the LORD his God. In everything
that he undertook in the service of God's temple
and in obedience to the law and the commands, he
sought his God and worked wholeheartedly. And so
he prospered.

2 Chronicles 31:20–21

You need to persevere so that when you have done the
will of God, you will receive what he has promised.

Hebrews 10:36

for men

Jesus said, "The kingdom of heaven is like treasure hidden in a field. When a man found it, he hid it again, and then in his joy went and sold all he had and bought that field."

Matthew 13:44

Run in such a way as to get the prize. Everyone who competes in the [Olympic] games goes into strict training. They do it to get a crown that will not last; but we do it to get a crown that will last forever.

1 Corinthians 9:24–25

Jesus said to his disciples, "If anyone would come after me, he must deny himself and take up his cross and follow me. For whoever wants to save his life will lose it, but whoever loses his life for me will find it."

Matthew 16:24–25

devotional thought
on commitment

"Give me liberty or give me death!" Patrick Henry spoke these words on March 23, 1775. He had made a decision that would shape the balance of his life as well as the history of the fledgling nation, and his fiery statement to his compatriots still rings in the ears of Americans today.

Joshua came to a similar place in his life. The tribes of Israel had returned to worshiping various false gods. Reminding the Israelites of God's central role in their history and their lives, Joshua called them to throw away their idols and serve God. Like Patrick Henry, Joshua's challenge to the Israelites still rings in the ears of Christians throughout the world today. His statement "As for me and my household, we will serve the LORD" (Joshua 24:15) has inspired millions to dedicate or rededicate their lives to following God's will and ways, no matter what the cost.

promises for life
on compassion

When Jesus landed and saw a large crowd, he had compassion on them, because they were like sheep without a shepherd.

Mark 6:34

Praise be to the God and Father of our Lord Jesus Christ, the Father of compassion and the God of all comfort, who comforts us in all our troubles, so that we can comfort those in any trouble with the comfort we ourselves have received from God. For just as the sufferings of Christ flow over into our lives, so also through Christ our comfort overflows.

2 Corinthians 1:3–5

Live in harmony with one another; be sympathetic, love as brothers, be compassionate and humble. Do not repay evil with evil or insult with insult, but with blessing, because to this you were called so that you may inherit a blessing.

1 Peter 3:8–9

Jesus said: "A man was going down from Jerusalem to Jericho, when he fell into the hands of robbers. They stripped him of his clothes, beat him and went away, leaving him half dead. A priest happened to be going down the same road, and when he saw the man, he passed by on the other side. So too, a Levite, when he came to the place and saw him, passed by on the other side. But a Samaritan, as he traveled, came where the man was; and when he saw him, he took pity on him. He went to him and bandaged his wounds.... Which of these three do you think was a neighbor to the man who fell into the hands of robbers?" The expert in the law replied, "The one who had mercy on him." Jesus told him, "Go and do likewise."

Luke 10:30–37

As God's chosen people, holy and dearly loved, clothe yourselves with compassion, kindness, humility, gentleness and patience.

Colossians 3:12

promises for life
on compassion

If you do away with the yoke of oppression,
    with the pointing finger and malicious talk,
and if you spend yourselves in behalf of the hungry
    and satisfy the needs of the oppressed,
then your light will rise in the darkness,
    and your night will become like the noonday.
The LORD will guide you always;
    he will satisfy your needs in a sun-scorched land
    and will strengthen your frame.
You will be like a well-watered garden,
    like a spring whose waters never fail.

Isaiah 58:9–11

Religion that God our Father accepts as pure and faultless is this: to look after orphans and widows in their distress.

James 1:27

This is what the LORD Almighty says: "Administer true justice; show mercy and compassion to one another. Do not oppress the widow or the fatherless, the alien or the poor."

Zechariah 7:9 – 10

This is how we know what love is: Jesus Christ laid down his life for us. And we ought to lay down our lives for our brothers. If anyone has material possessions and sees his brother in need but has no pity on him, how can the love of God be in him? Dear children, let us not love with words or tongue but with actions and in truth.

1 John 3:16 – 18

Defend the cause of the weak and fatherless;
    maintain the rights of the poor and oppressed.

Psalm 82:3

Look not only to your own interests, but also to the interests of others.

Philippians 2:4

for men

Then the King will say to those on his right, "Come, you who are blessed by my Father; take your inheritance, the kingdom prepared for you since the creation of the world. For I was hungry and you gave me something to eat, I was thirsty and you gave me something to drink, I was a stranger and you invited me in, I needed clothes and you clothed me, I was sick and you looked after me, I was in prison and you came to visit me." Then the righteous will answer him, "Lord, when did we see you hungry and feed you, or thirsty and give you something to drink?" … The King will reply, "I tell you the truth, whatever you did for one of the least of these brothers of mine, you did for me."

Matthew 25:34–40

devotional thought
on compassion

What we see can deceive us. First impressions often lie, because everyone has behind-the-scenes troubles we don't understand. In a culture that exalts image over substance, it goes against the grain to dig deeper. (How often in the course of a day do you ask someone "How are you?" hoping against hope that they don't want to give an honest answer?) But looking past appearances can reveal someone's long-buried needs or deepest desires.

We need to admit that we're not as good at reading people as we think. Then we must care enough to look harder and dig deeper. Those around us may be crying out without words. Ask God to help you see beyond the surface, beyond the frantic activity, and down to the heart to see the pain that your eye so easily misses. Then take the time to care, to listen, and to offer your help when it's needed.

promises for life
on contentment

Godliness with contentment is great gain. For we brought nothing into the world, and we can take nothing out of it. But if we have food and clothing, we will be content with that. People who want to get rich fall into temptation and a trap and into many foolish and harmful desires that plunge men into ruin and destruction. For the love of money is a root of all kinds of evil. Some people, eager for money, have wandered from the faith and pierced themselves with many griefs. But you, man of God, flee from all this, and pursue righteousness, godliness, faith, love, endurance and gentleness.

1 Timothy 6:6 – 11

Let the peace of Christ rule in your hearts, since as members of one body you were called to peace. And be thankful.

Colossians 3:15

This is the day the LORD has made;
    let us rejoice and be glad in it.

Psalm 118:24

The apostle Paul wrote, "I have learned to be content whatever the circumstances. I know what it is to be in need, and I know what it is to have plenty. I have learned the secret of being content in any and every situation, whether well fed or hungry, whether living in plenty or in want. I can do everything through him who gives me strength."

Philippians 4:11–13

Keep your lives free from the love of money and be content with what you have, because God has said,
    "Never will I leave you;
        never will I forsake you."

Hebrews 13:5

Be content with your pay.

Luke 3:14

37

promises for life
on contentment

"Come, all you who are thirsty,
   come to the waters;
and you who have no money,
   come, buy and eat!
Come, buy wine and milk
   without money and without cost.
Why spend money on what is not bread,
   and your labor on what does not satisfy?
Listen, listen to me, and eat what is good,
   and your soul will delight in the richest of fare,"
         declares the LORD.

Isaiah 55:1–2

Jesus said, "Peace I leave with you; my peace I give you."

John 14:27

May the righteous be glad
   and rejoice before God;
   may they be happy and joyful.

Psalm 68:3

The apostle Paul wrote, "Brothers, whatever is true, whatever is noble, whatever is right, whatever is pure, whatever is lovely, whatever is admirable—if anything is excellent or praiseworthy—think about such things. Whatever you have learned or received or heard from me, or seen in me—put it into practice. And the God of peace will be with you."

Philippians 4:8–9

Satisfy us in the morning with your unfailing love,
     O Lord,
    that we may sing for joy and be glad all our days.

Psalm 90:14

Jesus said, "Come to me, all you who are weary and burdened, and I will give you rest. Take my yoke upon you and learn from me, for I am gentle and humble in heart, and you will find rest for your souls. For my yoke is easy and my burden is light."

Matthew 11:28–30

for men

A happy heart makes the face cheerful.

Proverbs 15:13

He who dwells in the shelter of the Most High
will rest in the shadow of the Almighty.

Psalm 91:1

To the man who pleases him, God gives wisdom,
knowledge and happiness.

Ecclesiastes 2:26

Let all who take refuge in you be glad;
let them ever sing for joy.
Spread your protection over them,
that those who love your name may rejoice
in you.
For surely, O LORD, you bless the righteous;
you surround them with your favor as with
a shield.

Psalm 5:11–12

The fear of the LORD leads to life:
Then one rests content, untouched by trouble.

Proverbs 19:23

devotional thought
on contentment

A single mom shopping a week before Christmas summed up her spending spree: "I buy now and sort it out later. That's what credit cards are for." With two young kids, a huge mortgage, and a nanny to pay, this woman reflects the way a lot of us live—thinking just "one more thing" will make us happy.

So what does bring contentment? Paul said, "If we have food and clothing, we will be content with that" (1 Timothy 6:8). He knew that we can't find happiness in the stuff we collect or in the conditions around us.

We find contentment when we realize that knowing God and living for him brings true satisfaction, when we acknowledge that our relationship with Christ provides meaning and security in life. We find contentment when we understand that this relationship with Christ also assures us of eternal life—where even our deepest desires will be satisfied.

promises for life
on courage

The word of the LORD came to Abram in a vision:
"Do not be afraid, Abram.
I am your shield,
your very great reward."

Genesis 15:1

*Moses answered the people, "Do not be afraid. Stand
firm and you will see the deliverance the LORD will
bring you today.... The LORD will fight for you; you
need only to be still."*

Exodus 14:13–14

"Be still, and know that I am God;
I will be exalted among the nations,
I will be exalted in the earth."

Psalm 46:10

*Jesus said, "Are not two sparrows sold for a penny? Yet
not one of them will fall to the ground apart from the
will of your Father. And even the very hairs of your
head are all numbered. So don't be afraid; you are
worth more than many sparrows."*

Matthew 10:29–31

*Because the hand of the L*ORD *my God was on me, I took courage.*

Ezra 7:28

The battle is not yours, but God's.

2 Chronicles 20:15

*Be strong and courageous. Do not be terrified; do not be discouraged, for the L*ORD *your God will be with you wherever you go.*

Joshua 1:9

"Fear not, for I have redeemed you;
    I have summoned you by name; you are mine.
When you pass through the waters,
    I will be with you;
and when you pass through the rivers,
    they will not sweep over you.
When you walk through the fire,
    you will not be burned;
    the flames will not set you ablaze.
For I am the LORD, your God,
    the Holy One of Israel, your Savior."

Isaiah 43:1 – 3

promises for life
on courage

The LORD is my light and my salvation—
    whom shall I fear?
The LORD is the stronghold of my life—
    of whom shall I be afraid?

Psalm 27:1

I lift up my eyes to the hills—
    where does my help come from?
My help comes from the LORD,
    the Maker of heaven and earth.

Psalm 121:1–2

*Be on your guard; stand firm in the faith; be men of
courage; be strong.*

1 Corinthians 16:13

If you make the Most High your dwelling—
    even the LORD, who is my refuge—
then no harm will befall you,
    no disaster will come near your tent.
For he will command his angels concerning you
    to guard you in all your ways.

Psalm 91:9–11

Jesus said, "Don't be afraid; just believe."
Mark 5:36

God is our refuge and strength,
  an ever-present help in trouble.
Therefore we will not fear, though the earth give way
  and the mountains fall into the heart of the sea,
though its waters roar and foam
  and the mountains quake with their surging.
Psalm 46:1–3

My soul finds rest in God alone;
  my salvation comes from him.
He alone is my rock and my salvation;
  he is my fortress, I will never be shaken.
Psalm 62:1–2

Even though I walk
  through the valley of the shadow of death,
I will fear no evil,
  for you are with me, [O Lord];
your rod and your staff,
  they comfort me.
Psalm 23:4

45

for men

"Because he loves me," says the LORD, "I will
            rescue him;
      I will protect him, for he acknowledges
            my name.
He will call upon me, and I will answer him;
      I will be with him in trouble,
      I will deliver him and honor him.
With long life will I satisfy him
      and show him my salvation."

Psalm 91:14 – 16

*Jesus said, "Do not be afraid. I am the First and the
Last. I am the Living One; I was dead, and behold
I am alive for ever and ever! And I hold the keys of
death and Hades."*

Revelation 1:17 – 18

The LORD Almighty is with us;
      the God of Jacob is our fortress.

Psalm 46:11

devotional thought

on courage

The passengers who counterattacked the hijackers of United flight 93 on September 11, 2001, demonstrated that when a crisis strikes, ordinary people often rise to the occasion. The heroic actions of this group probably prevented the destruction of the U.S. Capitol or the White House.

In a taped phone conversation, Todd Beamer, one of the passengers, recited the Lord's Prayer and Psalm 23 and prayed, "Jesus, help me," before leading the attack on the hijackers. Undoubtedly, Beamer and his fellow passengers were scared. But faced with this challenge, his faith in Christ kicked in. He took action, uttering those now famous words, "Let's roll!"

Like Beamer's courageous call to action, Queen Esther's statement, "If I perish, I perish," perfectly expresses the do-or-die quality of active faith. Esther's decision to speak up on behalf of her threatened people, knowing that the king could execute her, shows that God provides courage in crisis to people willing to step out in faith.

promises for life
on eternal life

Jesus prayed, "This is eternal life: that they may know you, the only true God, and Jesus Christ, whom you have sent."

John 17:3

Jesus said, "I am the way and the truth and the life. No one comes to the Father except through me."

John 14:6

Jesus said, "God so loved the world that he gave his one and only Son, that whoever believes in him shall not perish but have eternal life. For God did not send his Son into the world to condemn the world, but to save the world through him."

John 3:16–17

Where sin increased, grace increased all the more, so that, just as sin reigned in death, so also grace might reign through righteousness to bring eternal life through Jesus Christ our Lord.

Romans 5:20–21

Whoever believes in the Son has eternal life.
John 3:36

Now that you have been set free from sin and have become slaves to God, the benefit you reap leads to holiness, and the result is eternal life. For the wages of sin is death, but the gift of God is eternal life in Christ Jesus our Lord.

Romans 6:22–23

Jesus said, "To him who overcomes, I will give the right to eat from the tree of life, which is in the paradise of God."

Revelation 2:7

Build yourselves up in your most holy faith and pray in the Holy Spirit. Keep yourselves in God's love as you wait for the mercy of our Lord Jesus Christ to bring you to eternal life.

Jude vv.20–21

promises for life
on eternal life

Jesus said, "Everyone who drinks this water will be thirsty again, but whoever drinks the water I give him will never thirst. Indeed, the water I give him will become in him a spring of water welling up to eternal life."

John 4:13–14

A man reaps what he sows. The one who sows to please his sinful nature, from that nature will reap destruction; the one who sows to please the Spirit, from the Spirit will reap eternal life.

Galatians 6:7–8

Jesus said, "I am the resurrection and the life. He who believes in me will live, even though he dies; and whoever lives and believes in me will never die."

John 11:25–26

God "will give to each person according to what he has done." To those who by persistence in doing good seek glory, honor and immortality, he will give eternal life.

Romans 2:6–7

Jesus said, "Whoever hears my word and believes him who sent me has eternal life and will not be condemned; he has crossed over from death to life."

John 5:24

Fight the good fight of the faith. Take hold of the eternal life to which you were called.

1 Timothy 6:12

Jesus declared, "I tell you the truth, no one can see the kingdom of God unless he is born again."

John 3:3

This is the testimony: God has given us eternal life, and this life is in his Son. He who has the Son has life.

1 John 5:11–12

Jesus said, "My sheep listen to my voice; I know them, and they follow me. I give them eternal life, and they shall never perish."

John 10:27–28

for men

Jesus declared, "My Father's will is that everyone who looks to the Son and believes in him shall have eternal life, and I will raise him up at the last day."

John 6:40

Jesus did many other miraculous signs in the presence of his disciples, which are not recorded in this book. But these are written that you may believe that Jesus is the Christ, the Son of God, and that by believing you may have life in his name.

John 20:30–31

Jesus said, "I am the bread of life. Your forefathers ate the manna in the desert, yet they died. But here is the bread that comes down from heaven, which a man may eat and not die. I am the living bread that came down from heaven. If anyone eats of this bread, he will live forever."

John 6:48–51

devotional thought
on eternal life

Ah, the finish line! It makes all the pain bearable. Joy fills your heart as you see the tape stretched across the journey's end. Every last ounce of strength drives you across the finish line.

Jesus understood that intense drive to finish. With one of his last breaths, he cried out, "It is finished!" In the language of the New Testament, that's a one-word exclamation: "Done!"

Jesus had joined the human race for a specific reason—to finish God's plan to provide forgiveness, salvation, and eternal life for a fallen humanity. When Jesus shouted, "Finished!" he endured the judgment of sin on behalf of all mankind.

The cross represented the last hours in a long race marked out for Jesus. He knew that many would never accept his sacrifice, but he also knew that many would, and for us, he ran. And he finished. And for this, we'll spend eternity in grateful appreciation.

promises for life
on faithfulness

Let those who love the LORD hate evil,
     for he guards the lives of his faithful ones
     and delivers them from the hand of the wicked.
Light is shed upon the righteous
     and joy on the upright in heart.
Rejoice in the LORD, you who are righteous,
     and praise his holy name.

Psalm 97:10–12

*This man was blameless and upright; he feared God
and shunned evil.*

Job 1:1

Blessed are all who fear the LORD,
     who walk in his ways.
You will eat the fruit of your labor;
     blessings and prosperity will be yours.
Your wife will be like a fruitful vine
     within your house;
your sons will be like olive shoots
     around your table.
Thus is the man blessed
     who fears the LORD.

Psalm 128:1–4

for men

Blessed is the man
>   who does not walk in the counsel of the wicked
or stand in the way of sinners
>   or sit in the seat of mockers.
But his delight is in the law of the LORD,
>   and on his law he meditates day and night.
He is like a tree planted by streams of water,
>   which yields its fruit in season
and whose leaf does not wither.
>   Whatever he does prospers.

Psalm 1:1–3

"My eyes will be on the faithful in the land,
>   that they may dwell with me,"
>   declares the LORD.

Psalm 101:6

*The LORD rewards every man for his righteousness
and faithfulness.*

1 Samuel 26:23

Consider the blameless, observe the upright;
>   there is a future for the man of peace.

Psalm 37:37

promises for life
on faithfulness

To the faithful you show yourself faithful, [O LORD].
2 Samuel 22:26

Jesus said, "Whoever acknowledges me before men, I will also acknowledge him before my Father in heaven."

Matthew 10:32

The righteous are as bold as a lion.

Proverbs 28:1

Let love and faithfulness never leave you;
    bind them around your neck,
    write them on the tablet of your heart.
Then you will win favor and a good name
    in the sight of God and man.

Proverbs 3:3 – 4

My heart is steadfast, O God,
    my heart is steadfast.

Psalm 57:7

Fear the LORD and serve him with all faithfulness.

Joshua 24:14

A faithful man will be richly blessed.

Proverbs 28:20

Blessed is the man who fears the LORD,
    who finds great delight in his commands.
His children will be mighty in the land;
    the generation of the upright will be blessed.
Wealth and riches are in his house,
    and his righteousness endures forever.
Even in darkness light dawns for the upright,
    for the gracious and compassionate and
        righteous man.
Good will come to him who is generous and
        lends freely,
    who conducts his affairs with justice.
Surely he will never be shaken;
    a righteous man will be remembered forever.
He will have no fear of bad news;
    his heart is steadfast, trusting in the LORD.

Psalm 112:1–7

*Jotham grew powerful because he walked steadfastly
before the LORD his God.*

2 Chronicles 27:6

Love the LORD, all his saints!
>   The LORD preserves the faithful.

Psalm 31:23

The LORD loves the just
>   and will not forsake his faithful ones.

Psalm 37:28

Jesus said, "Be faithful, even to the point of death, and I will give you the crown of life."

Revelation 2:10

Create in me a pure heart, O God,
>   and renew a steadfast spirit within me.
Do not cast me from your presence
>   or take your Holy Spirit from me.
Restore to me the joy of your salvation
>   and grant me a willing spirit, to sustain me.

Psalm 51:10–12

Jesus said, "You will receive power when the Holy Spirit comes on you; and you will be my witnesses in Jerusalem, and in all Judea and Samaria, and to the ends of the earth."

Acts 1:8

devotional thought
on faithfulness

At a well-known company's national sales convention, a heralded speaker delivered a stirring motivational talk. However, he frequently used God's name in vain. Finally, an unknown Christian salesman shouted, "Please leave God out of it." The speaker cleaned up the rest of his speech. But after the session, more people waited in line to shake the Christian man's hand than the speaker's.

The leaders of the infant church displayed even greater courage. These "ordinary" men stood toe to toe with political and religious forces that sought to silence them. They didn't cower, give in, or give up. Instead, they stood bold and heroic, astonishing their adversaries, who knew only that these men had been with Jesus.

Speaking valiantly for Christ and courageously living a righteous life requires living out our convictions and commitments as faithful men. We can only prepare for the battle by spending time with Jesus—the unshakeable source of courage.

promises for life
on forgiveness

*[God] passed in front of Moses, proclaiming,
"The LORD, the LORD, the compassionate and
gracious God, slow to anger, abounding in love and
faithfulness, maintaining love to thousands, and
forgiving wickedness, rebellion and sin."*

Exodus 34:6–7

You are forgiving and good, O Lord,
    abounding in love to all who call to you.

Psalm 86:5

*If we confess our sins, [God] is faithful and just
and will forgive us our sins and purify us from all
unrighteousness.*

1 John 1:9

*Be kind and compassionate to one another, forgiving
each other, just as in Christ God forgave you.*

Ephesians 4:32

*Jesus said, "Do not judge, and you will not be judged.
Do not condemn, and you will not be condemned.
Forgive, and you will be forgiven."*

Luke 6:37

Jesus said, "If your brother sins, rebuke him, and if he repents, forgive him. If he sins against you seven times in a day, and seven times comes back to you and says, "I repent," forgive him."

Luke 17:3–4

Peter came to Jesus and asked, "Lord, how many times shall I forgive my brother when he sins against me? Up to seven times?" Jesus answered, "I tell you, not seven times, but seventy-seven times."

Matthew 18:21–22

As God's chosen people, holy and dearly loved, clothe yourselves with compassion, kindness, humility, gentleness and patience. Bear with each other and forgive whatever grievances you may have against one another. Forgive as the Lord forgave you. And over all these virtues put on love, which binds them all together in perfect unity.

Colossians 3:12–14

Jesus said, "If you forgive men when they sin against you, your heavenly Father will also forgive you."

Matthew 6:14

for men

Jesus said, "When you stand praying, if you hold anything against anyone, forgive him, so that your Father in heaven may forgive you your sins."

Mark 11:25

Jesus said, "If you are offering your gift at the altar and there remember that your brother has something against you, leave your gift there in front of the altar. First go and be reconciled to your brother; then come and offer your gift."

Matthew 5:23–24

Jesus said, "Forgive us our sins, O LORD, for we also forgive everyone who sins against us."

Luke 11:4

Jesus said, "If you forgive anyone his sins, they are forgiven."

John 20:23

In [Christ] we have redemption through his blood, the forgiveness of sins, in accordance with the riches of God's grace.

Ephesians 1:7

devotional thought
on forgiveness

When a loud knock interrupts a quiet evening, you open the door to find your neighbor standing there. You stiffen and step back slightly. He says, "I realize I've been a jerk as a neighbor. I'd like to do a lot better from here on out. Will you forgive me?"

That kind of a turnaround is a bit like what happened with King Ahab and Elijah.

King Ahab hated Elijah. Every time Elijah opened his mouth, Ahab heard God speak, and he despised the message. However, something in Elijah's message this time got Ahab's attention. Ahab repented.

How do you think Elijah felt? Could he forgive Ahab?

Forgiveness seems like a great idea until we actually have to do it. Then it's just hard. Perhaps we can't play the part of the neighbor who forgives until we know what it's like to be the neighbor standing outside about to say, "Will you forgive me?"

promises for life
on friends

Jonathan became one in spirit with David, and he loved him as himself.

1 Samuel 18:1

I am a friend to all who fear you, O LORD,
    to all who follow your precepts.

Psalm 119:63

As iron sharpens iron,
    so one man sharpens another.

Proverbs 27:17

Do not make friends with a hot-tempered man,
    do not associate with one easily angered,
or you may learn his ways
    and get yourself ensnared.

Proverbs 22:24–25

He who loves a pure heart and whose speech
        is gracious
    will have the king for his friend.

Proverbs 22:11

Keep on loving each other as brothers.

Hebrews 13:1

Jonathan said to David, "Go in peace, for we have sworn friendship with each other in the name of the LORD, saying, 'The LORD is witness between you and me, and between your descendants and my descendants forever.'"

1 Samuel 20:42

The pleasantness of one's friend springs from his earnest counsel.

Proverbs 27:9

A righteous man is cautious in friendship.

Proverbs 12:26

Wealth brings many friends,
    but a poor man's friend deserts him.

Proverbs 19:4

Bad company corrupts good character.

1 Corinthians 15:33

He who walks with the wise grows wise,
    but a companion of fools suffers harm.

Proverbs 13:20

The apostle Paul wrote, "He is very dear to me ... both as a man and as a brother in the Lord."

Philemon 1:16

A friend loves at all times.

Proverbs 17:17

Do not be yoked together with unbelievers. For what do righteousness and wickedness have in common? Or what fellowship can light have with darkness?

2 Corinthians 6:14

A man of many companions may come to ruin,
   but there is a friend who sticks closer than
      a brother.

Proverbs 18:24

Wounds from a friend can be trusted.

Proverbs 27:6

Do not forsake your friend.

Proverbs 27:10

Jesus said, "Greater love has no one than this, that he lay down his life for his friends."

John 15:13

devotional thought
on friends

God wants us to form our closest friendships with people who hold values that are in line with God's character. People who are headed for the same direction in life. People who love God and help us love him better.

If the phrase "you are who your friends are" reflects the truth, what do your friends say about who you are? If you've hung onto a friend who drags you down spiritually, maybe you need to set some new boundaries. Make it your goal to change that relationship, either by making a new effort to influence this friend for Christ or to cut down on your association with him.

Perhaps you simply need to invest in new friends who share your core beliefs. Initiating deeper friendships with other men who love Christ is never easy. We're guys, after all. But if you're persistent, your efforts will pay rich dividends.

promises for life
on giftedness

The LORD said to Moses, "See, I have chosen Bezalel son of Uri, the son of Hur, of the tribe of Judah, and I have filled him with the Spirit of God, with skill, ability and knowledge in all kinds of crafts — to make artistic designs for work in gold, silver and bronze, to cut and set stones, to work in wood, and to engage in all kinds of craftsmanship."

Exodus 31:1–5

We have different gifts, according to the grace given us. If a man's gift is prophesying, let him use it in proportion to his faith. If it is serving, let him serve; if it is teaching, let him teach; if it is encouraging, let him encourage; if it is contributing to the needs of others, let him give generously; if it is leadership, let him govern diligently; if it is showing mercy, let him do it cheerfully.

Romans 12:6–8

In the church God has appointed first of all apostles, second prophets, third teachers, then workers of miracles, also those having gifts of healing, those able to help others, those with gifts of administration, and those speaking in different kinds of tongues.

1 Corinthians 12:28

To each one of us grace has been given as Christ apportioned it. This is why it says:
> *"When he ascended on high,*
> *he led captives in his train*
> *and gave gifts to men."*
… It was he who gave some to be apostles, some to be prophets, some to be evangelists, and some to be pastors and teachers, to prepare God's people for works of service, so that the body of Christ may be built up until we all reach unity in the faith and in the knowledge of the Son of God and become mature, attaining to the whole measure of the fullness of Christ.

Ephesians 4:7–8, 11–13

for men

Bless all his skills, O LORD,
> and be pleased with the work of his hands.

Deuteronomy 33:11

To each one the manifestation of the Spirit is given for the common good. To one there is given through the Spirit the message of wisdom, to another the message of knowledge by means of the same Spirit, to another faith by the same Spirit, to another gifts of healing by that one Spirit, to another miraculous powers, to another prophecy, to another distinguishing between spirits, to another speaking in different kinds of tongues, and to still another the interpretation of tongues. All these are the work of one and the same Spirit, and he gives them to each one, just as he determines.

1 Corinthians 12:7–11

God's gifts and his call are irrevocable.

Romans 11:29

devotional thought
on giftedness

A farmer looked up and saw the letters "PC" in the clouds. Thinking this was a sign from God to "preach Christ," he left his tractor and enrolled in seminary. But he struggled in his coursework and, frustrated, turned to his advisor and told him about the vision he had. His advisor said, "Son, did you ever think that 'PC' might have meant 'plant corn'?"

When God chooses us to do something, it's as if he created us specifically for a task—just like he created fish to swim and birds to fly. God calls some of us to be students, some teachers. He calls some to be fathers, some single. He calls some to Christian service in ministries, some to public service in government.

God has gifted you with special talents, insight, wisdom, and passions. He created you to accomplish exactly what he needs you to do for him in this world.

promises for life
on gratitude

Thanks be to God for his indescribable gift!
                                    2 Corinthians 9:15

Come, let us sing for joy to the LORD;
    let us shout aloud to the Rock of our salvation.
Let us come before him with thanksgiving
    and extol him with music and song.
                                    Psalm 95:1–2

Be thankful. Let the word of Christ dwell in you richly as you teach and admonish one another with all wisdom, and as you sing psalms, hymns and spiritual songs with gratitude in your hearts to God. And whatever you do, whether in word or deed, do it all in the name of the Lord Jesus, giving thanks to God the Father through him.
                                    Colossians 3:15–17

Praise be to the LORD,
> for he has heard my cry for mercy.
The LORD is my strength and my shield;
> my heart trusts in him, and I am helped.
My heart leaps for joy
> and I will give thanks to him in song.

Psalm 28:6–7

Sing and make music in your heart to the Lord,
always giving thanks to God the Father for
everything, in the name of our Lord Jesus Christ.

Ephesians 5:19–20

Enter his gates with thanksgiving
> and his courts with praise;
> give thanks to him and praise his name.
For the LORD is good and his love endures forever;
> his faithfulness continues through
> all generations.

Psalm 100:4–5

promises for life
on gratitude

*Rejoice in the Lord always. I will say it again: Rejoice!
Let your gentleness be evident to all. The Lord is near.
Do not be anxious about anything, but in everything,
by prayer and petition, with thanksgiving, present
your requests to God.*

Philippians 4:4–6

Now, our God, we give you thanks,
    and praise your glorious name.

1 Chronicles 29:13

*Be joyful always; pray continually; give thanks in
all circumstances, for this is God's will for you in
Christ Jesus.*

1 Thessalonians 5:16–18

Let them give thanks to the LORD for his
                unfailing love
    and his wonderful deeds for men,
for he satisfies the thirsty
        and fills the hungry with good things.

Psalm 107:8–9

We pray this in order that you may live a life worthy of the Lord and may please him in every way: bearing fruit in every good work, growing in the knowledge of God, being strengthened with all power according to his glorious might so that you may have great endurance and patience, and joyfully giving thanks to the Father, who has qualified you to share in the inheritance of the saints in the kingdom of light.

Colossians 1:10–12

Give thanks to the LORD, for he is good;
    his love endures forever.

1 Chronicles 16:34

Since we are receiving a kingdom that cannot be shaken, let us be thankful, and so worship God acceptably with reverence and awe.

Hebrews 12:28

Thanks be to God! He gives us the victory through our Lord Jesus Christ.

1 Corinthians 15:57

for men

Give thanks to the LORD, call on his name;
> make known among the nations what he
>> has done.
Sing to him, sing praise to him;
> tell of all his wonderful acts.

1 Chronicles 16:8–9

Just as you received Christ Jesus as Lord, continue to live in him, rooted and built up in him, strengthened in the faith as you were taught, and overflowing with thankfulness.

Colossians 2:6–7

I will give thanks to the LORD
> because of his righteousness
and will sing praise to the name
> of the LORD Most High.

Psalm 7:17

*Praise and glory
and wisdom and thanks and honor
and power and strength
be to our God for ever and ever.*

Revelation 7:12

devotional thought
on gratitude

When King Solomon was just beginning his reign over Israel, he unexpectedly experienced God's presence while praying outside the temple. Solomon's immediate response was unbridled thankfulness and joy—a joy so great that the king called for a raucous, nationwide fifteen-day festival of celebration and dedication to God!

Probably the closest modern parallel we might have to this event is the American celebration of Thanksgiving. That too is a nationally mandated day of rest and reflection, a time to gather together with friends and family and to give thanks to God for his goodness throughout the year. Imagine the president mandating that all of America celebrate this festival for two solid weeks. The damage to the checkbook and the waistline would be impressive.

For the Christian, every single day is Thanksgiving Day, a day to celebrate what God is doing in your life and to reflect on his goodness and grace.

promises for life
on grief

Blessed are those who mourn,
for they will be comforted.

Matthew 5:4

I cried like a swift or thrush,
I moaned like a mourning dove.
My eyes grew weak as I looked to the heavens.
I am troubled; O Lord, come to my aid!

Isaiah 38:14

You, O God, do see trouble and grief;
you consider it to take it in hand.

Psalm 10:14

The LORD will be your everlasting light,
and your days of sorrow will end.

Isaiah 60:20

Those who sow in tears
will reap with songs of joy.
He who goes out weeping,
carrying seed to sow,
will return with songs of joy,
carrying sheaves with him.

Psalm 126:5–6

Weeping may remain for a night,
    but rejoicing comes in the morning.

Psalm 30:5

Be merciful to me, O LORD, for I am in distress;
    my eyes grow weak with sorrow,
    my soul and my body with grief.

Psalm 31:9

May your unfailing love be my comfort, [O LORD],
    according to your promise.

Psalm 119:76

Brothers, we do not want you to be ignorant about those who fall asleep, or to grieve like the rest of men, who have no hope. We believe that Jesus died and rose again and so we believe that God will bring with Jesus those who have fallen asleep in him.

1 Thessalonians 4:13–14

"As a mother comforts her child,
    so will I comfort you,"
    declares the LORD.

Isaiah 66:13

promises for life
on grief

My soul is weary with sorrow, [O LORD];
    strengthen me according to your word.

Psalm 119:28

The Spirit of the Sovereign LORD is on me,
    because the LORD has anointed me
    to preach good news to the poor.
He has sent me to bind up the brokenhearted,
    to proclaim freedom for the captives
    and release from darkness for the prisoners,
to proclaim the year of the LORD's favor
    and the day of vengeance of our God,
to comfort all who mourn,
    and provide for those who grieve in Zion—
to bestow on them a crown of beauty
    instead of ashes,
the oil of gladness
    instead of mourning,
and a garment of praise
    instead of a spirit of despair.

Isaiah 61:1–3

O my Comforter in sorrow,
my heart is faint within me.

Jeremiah 8:18

There is a time for everything,
and a season for every activity under heaven:
a time to be born and a time to die,
a time to plant and a time to uproot,
a time to kill and a time to heal,
a time to tear down and a time to build,
a time to weep and a time to laugh,
a time to mourn and a time to dance.

Ecclesiastes 3:1 – 4

God, who comforts the downcast, comforted us.

2 Corinthians 7:6

"I will turn their mourning into gladness;
I will give them comfort and joy instead
of sorrow,"

declares the LORD.

Jeremiah 31:13

for men

The ransomed of the LORD will return.
They will enter Zion with singing;
everlasting joy will crown their heads.
Gladness and joy will overtake them,
and sorrow and sighing will flee away.

Isaiah 51:11

Praise be to the God and Father of our Lord Jesus Christ, the Father of compassion and the God of all comfort, who comforts us in all our troubles, so that we can comfort those in any trouble with the comfort we ourselves have received from God. For just as the sufferings of Christ flow over into our lives, so also through Christ our comfort overflows.

2 Corinthians 1:3–5

Mourn with those who mourn.

Romans 12:15

[God] will wipe every tear from their eyes. There will be no more death or mourning or crying or pain, for the old order of things has passed away.

Revelation 21:4

devotional thought
on grief

Death doesn't dash our hope in Christ; indeed, death for Christians marks a transition to a much better life.

Paul reminds us that we don't need to grieve the death of our loved ones or worry about our own deaths like "the rest of men" (1 Thessalonians 4:13). Notice that Paul doesn't say that Christians won't grieve. Death is horrible, and it separates us from our loved ones. If we tried to pretend that this loss didn't matter, we wouldn't be authentic.

Paul, instead, wants us to know that we don't need to grieve like those without hope. Yes, we grieve our loss, but we also rejoice knowing that one day we'll reunite with loved ones who also knew Christ. More importantly, Christ will unite us with himself for all eternity.

on hope

I know that my Redeemer lives.

Job 19:25

Blessed is the man who trusts in the LORD,
    whose confidence is in him.
He will be like a tree planted by the water
    that sends out its roots by the stream.
It does not fear when heat comes;
    its leaves are always green.
It has no worries in a year of drought
    and never fails to bear fruit.

Jeremiah 17:7–8

Be strong and take heart,
    all you who hope in the LORD.

Psalm 31:24

*May the God of hope fill you with all joy and peace as
you trust in him, so that you may overflow with hope
by the power of the Holy Spirit.*

Romans 15:13

Why are you downcast, O my soul?
    Why so disturbed within me?
Put your hope in God,
    for I will yet praise him,
    my Savior and my God.

Psalm 42:11

The eyes of the LORD are on those who fear him,
    on those whose hope is in his unfailing love.

Psalm 33:18

Find rest, O my soul, in God alone;
    my hope comes from him.
He alone is my rock and my salvation;
    he is my fortress, I will not be shaken.
My salvation and my honor depend on God;
    he is my mighty rock, my refuge.
Trust in him at all times, O people;
    pour out your hearts to him,
    for God is our refuge.

Psalm 62:5 – 8

promises for life
on hope

Blessed is he whose help is the God of Jacob,
    whose hope is in the LORD his God,
the Maker of heaven and earth,
    the sea, and everything in them.

Psalm 146:5–6

We wait in hope for the LORD;
    he is our help and our shield.
In him our hearts rejoice,
    for we trust in his holy name.
May your unfailing love rest upon us, O LORD,
    even as we put our hope in you.

Psalm 33:20–22

You have been my hope, O Sovereign LORD,
    my confidence since my youth.

Psalm 71:5

No one whose hope is in you [O LORD]
    will ever be put to shame.

Psalm 25:3

You are God my Savior,
    and my hope is in you all day long.

Psalm 25:5

*Such confidence as this is ours through Christ
before God.*

2 Corinthians 3:4

I trust in God's unfailing love
    for ever and ever.
I will praise you forever for what you have done;
    in your name I will hope, for your name is good.
    I will praise you in the presence of your saints.

Psalm 52:8–9

Guard my life and rescue me;
    let me not be put to shame,
    for I take refuge in you.
May integrity and uprightness protect me,
    because my hope is in you.

Psalm 25:20–21

for men

Do not throw away your confidence; it will be richly rewarded. You need to persevere so that when you have done the will of God, you will receive what he has promised.

Hebrews 10:35–36

I wait for the LORD, my soul waits,
    and in his word I put my hope.
My soul waits for the Lord
    more than watchmen wait for the morning.

Psalm 130:5–6

It is God who makes both us and you stand firm in Christ. He anointed us, set his seal of ownership on us, and put his Spirit in our hearts as a deposit, guaranteeing what is to come.

2 Corinthians 1:21–22

Always be prepared to give an answer to everyone who asks you to give the reason for the hope that you have.

1 Peter 3:15

devotional thought
on hope

According to *The Worst-Case Scenario Survival Handbook*, to escape from a bear you lie still, and if attacked, fight back. Helpful, huh?

Perhaps what we need is a book about getting out of common, real-life dead ends. That Table of Contents might include, "How to survive an unexpected layoff."

Actually, the Bible puts more emphasis on *God's* rescuing us than on our exiting from dead ends in our own strength. When the Hebrews saw the sea in front of them and the Egyptian army at their back, God opened up the sea. When Daniel spent the night in the lions' den, God gave the lions the disposition of kittens.

Sometimes you find yourself in circumstances where only he can rescue you. No matter what you're going through, hold on. Don't give up hope. God can bring you out.

promises for life
on humility

Humility and the fear of the LORD
  bring wealth and honor and life.

Proverbs 22:4

Humble yourselves before the Lord, and he will lift you up.

James 4:10

The meek will inherit the land
  and enjoy great peace.

Psalm 37:11

The LORD sustains the humble.

Psalm 147:6

Do nothing out of selfish ambition or vain conceit, but in humility consider others better than yourselves.

Philippians 2:3

Though the LORD is on high, he looks upon the lowly.

Psalm 138:6

Be completely humble and gentle; be patient, bearing with one another in love.

Ephesians 4:2

Good and upright is the LORD;
   therefore he instructs sinners in his ways.
He guides the humble in what is right
   and teaches them his way.

Psalm 25:8–9

*Do not think of yourself more highly than you ought,
but rather think of yourself with sober judgment,
in accordance with the measure of faith God has
given you.*

Romans 12:3

*God chose the foolish things of the world to shame
the wise; God chose the weak things of the world to
shame the strong. He chose the lowly things of this
world and the despised things — and the things that
are not — to nullify the things that are, so that no one
may boast before him. It is because of him that you
are in Christ Jesus, who has become for us wisdom
from God — that is, our righteousness, holiness and
redemption. Therefore, as it is written: "Let him who
boasts boast in the Lord."*

1 Corinthians 1:27–31

The LORD takes delight in his people;
>   he crowns the humble with salvation.

Psalm 149:4

With humility comes wisdom.

Proverbs 11:2

When [Jesus] noticed how the guests picked the places of honor at the table, he told them this parable: "When someone invites you to a wedding feast, do not take the place of honor, for a person more distinguished than you may have been invited. If so, the host who invited both of you will come and say to you, 'Give this man your seat.' Then, humiliated, you will have to take the least important place. But when you are invited, take the lowest place, so that when your host comes, he will say to you, 'Friend, move up to a better place.' Then you will be honored in the presence of all your fellow guests. For everyone who exalts himself will be humbled, and he who humbles himself will be exalted."

Luke 14:7–11

devotional thought
on humility

The box holding a diamond engagement ring isn't meant to draw attention to itself. The box exists solely to make the ring look good. Inside, the ring tucks into white satin or black velvet to allow the beauty of the diamond to shine.

When Paul says that "we have this treasure in jars of clay" (2 Corinthians 4:7), he means that we're ordinary vessels, not ornate glass vases. In other words, Paul urges us not to live in a way that draws attention to ourselves. Instead, we should seek to show the shining brilliance of the One who lives within us.

The apostle Paul existed to make Jesus look good. As he sought to bring people to Christ, Paul didn't want them to overlook Christ and fall in love with Paul instead. What a goal! Might we also simply be jars of clay, desiring only to attract people to the treasure we hold inside.

promises for life
on identity

How great is the love the Father has lavished on us, that we should be called children of God! And that is what we are!

1 John 3:1

Praise be to the God and Father of our Lord Jesus Christ, who has blessed us in the heavenly realms with every spiritual blessing in Christ. For he chose us in him before the creation of the world to be holy and blameless in his sight. In love he predestined us to be adopted as his sons through Jesus Christ, in accordance with his pleasure and will.

Ephesians 1:3–5

Both the one who makes men holy and those who are made holy are of the same family. So Jesus is not ashamed to call them brothers.

Hebrews 2:11

You are all sons of God through faith in Christ Jesus, for all of you who were baptized into Christ have clothed yourselves with Christ. There is neither Jew nor Greek, slave nor free, male nor female, for you are all one in Christ Jesus. If you belong to Christ, then you are Abraham's seed, and heirs according to the promise.

Galatians 3:26–29

Consider Abraham: "He believed God, and it was credited to him as righteousness." Understand, then, that those who believe are children of Abraham. The Scripture foresaw that God would justify the Gentiles by faith, and announced the gospel in advance to Abraham: "All nations will be blessed through you." So those who have faith are blessed along with Abraham, the man of faith.

Galatians 3:6–9

promises for life
on identity

God sent his Son, born of a woman, born under law, to redeem those under law, that we might receive the full rights of sons. Because you are sons, God sent the Spirit of his Son into our hearts, the Spirit who calls out, "Abba, Father." So you are no longer a slave, but a son; and since you are a son, God has made you also an heir.

Galatians 4:4–7

You were once darkness, but now you are light in the Lord. Live as children of light.

Ephesians 5:8

You are a chosen people, a royal priesthood, a holy nation, a people belonging to God, that you may declare the praises of him who called you out of darkness into his wonderful light.

1 Peter 2:9

You created my inmost being, [O LORD];
    you knit me together in my mother's womb.
I praise you because I am fearfully and wonderfully
            made;
    your works are wonderful,
    I know that full well.
My frame was not hidden from you
    when I was made in the secret place.
When I was woven together in the depths of
            the earth,
    your eyes saw my unformed body.
All the days ordained for me
    were written in your book
    before one of them came to be.

Psalm 139:13–16

Come, let us bow down in worship,
    let us kneel before the LORD our Maker;
for he is our God
    and we are the people of his pasture,
    the flock under his care.

Psalm 95:6–7

for men

"Fear not, for I have redeemed you;
    I have summoned you by name; you are mine,"
        declares the LORD.

Isaiah 43:1

Jesus said, "I no longer call you servants, because a servant does not know his master's business. Instead, I have called you friends, for everything that I learned from my Father I have made known to you."

John 15:15

Jesus said, "You are the light of the world. A city on a hill cannot be hidden. Neither do people light a lamp and put it under a bowl. Instead they put it on its stand, and it gives light to everyone in the house. In the same way, let your light shine before men, that they may see your good deeds and praise your Father in heaven."

Matthew 5:14–16

You are the body of Christ, and each one of you is a part of it.

1 Corinthians 12:27

devotional thought
on identity

Many men allow their career to define who they are as a person, and how others perceive them. We use other ways to define ourselves as well—family pedigree, the behavior of our kids, our educational background, or our physical abilities.

When Jeremiah encourages the people of Judah to abandon their idolatrous lifestyles and return to God, he asks why they would look to idols for strength, comfort, and guidance. Such a pursuit yields the same results as trying to draw water from a leaky cistern.

Similarly, when we define ourselves by career, family ties, athletic ability, or any other achievement, we draw water from a leaky cistern. We make those achievements into idols. In fact, looking to anything or anyone except God for our ultimate identity constitutes idolatry. But when we base our identity on the God who loves us, we drink from the spring of living water.

Two are better than one,
> because they have a good return for their work:
If one falls down,
> his friend can help him up.
But pity the man who falls
> and has no one to help him up!

Ecclesiastes 4:9–10

Let us consider how we may spur one another on toward love and good deeds. Let us not give up meeting together, as some are in the habit of doing, but let us encourage one another.

Hebrews 10:24–25

As iron sharpens iron,
> so one man sharpens another.

Proverbs 27:17

Encourage one another and build each other up.

1 Thessalonians 5:11

Brothers, if someone is caught in a sin, you who are spiritual should restore him gently. But watch yourself, or you also may be tempted. Carry each other's burdens, and in this way you will fulfill the law of Christ.

Galatians 6:1–2

Respect those who work hard among you, who are over you in the Lord and who admonish you. Hold them in the highest regard in love because of their work.

1 Thessalonians 5:12–13

Obey your leaders and submit to their authority. They keep watch over you as men who must give an account. Obey them so that their work will be a joy, not a burden, for that would be of no advantage to you.

Hebrews 13:17

promises for life
on individualism

Jesus said, "My command is this: Love each other as I have loved you. Greater love has no one than this, that he lay down his life for his friends."

John 15:12–13

This is how we know what love is: Jesus Christ laid down his life for us. And we ought to lay down our lives for our brothers. If anyone has material possessions and sees his brother in need but has no pity on him, how can the love of God be in him? Dear children, let us not love with words or tongue but with actions and in truth.

1 John 3:16–18

Be devoted to one another in brotherly love.

Romans 12:10

Each of you should look not only to your own interests, but also to the interests of others.

Philippians 2:4

The apostle Paul wrote, "I long to see you so that I may impart to you some spiritual gift to make you strong — that is, that you and I may be mutually encouraged by each other's faith."

Romans 1:11–12

There is a friend who sticks closer than a brother.

Proverbs 18:24

Confess your sins to each other and pray for each other so that you may be healed.

James 5:16

Let the word of Christ dwell in you richly as you teach and admonish one another with all wisdom.

Colossians 3:16

Encourage one another daily, as long as it is called Today, so that none of you may be hardened by sin's deceitfulness.

Hebrews 3:13

for men

My brothers, if one of you should wander from the truth and someone should bring him back, remember this: Whoever turns a sinner from the error of his way will save him from death and cover over a multitude of sins.

James 5:19–20

Warn those who are idle, encourage the timid, help the weak, be patient with everyone. Make sure that nobody pays back wrong for wrong, but always try to be kind to each other and to everyone else.

1 Thessalonians 5:14–15

If we walk in the light, as [God] is in the light, we have fellowship with one another, and the blood of Jesus, his Son, purifies us from all sin.

1 John 1:7

Though one may be overpowered,
    two can defend themselves.
A cord of three strands is not quickly broken.

Ecclesiastes 4:12

devotional thought
on individualism

A lot of us guys assume that being a man requires handling life on our own. This distorted view of independence makes sense when we look at our boyhood heroes — John Wayne, Clint Eastwood, the Lone Ranger, Han Solo.

Ezekiel reminds us that we face a true spiritual battle, and — whether or not we want to admit it — that we need help on the battlefield.

Just as God places Ezekiel on guard to stand watch over Israel, so we also need friends who care about us to stand watch in our lives.

A friend standing watch senses when you're going through a tough time and offers words of hope. He confronts you when you spend too much time with people who are bad influences. He finds ways to help you reach your goals. Ultimately, you hope that the friend you ask to stand guard in your life will always guide you back to God.

promises for life
on integrity

They came to [Jesus] and said, "Teacher, we know you are a man of integrity. You aren't swayed by men, because you pay no attention to who they are."

Mark 12:14

May integrity and uprightness protect me,
    because my hope is in you [O LORD].

Psalm 25:21

My shield is God Most High,
    who saves the upright in heart.

Psalm 7:10

In my integrity you uphold me, [O LORD,]
    and set me in your presence forever.

Psalm 41:12

The LORD is righteous,
    he loves justice;
    upright men will see his face.

Psalm 11:7

Kings take pleasure in honest lips;
    they value a man who speaks the truth.

Proverbs 16:13

*I know, my God, that you test the heart and are
pleased with integrity.*

1 Chronicles 29:17

The integrity of the upright guides them.

Proverbs 11:3

Better is one day in your courts, [O LORD,]
    than a thousand elsewhere;
I would rather be a doorkeeper in the house of
            my God
    than dwell in the tents of the wicked.
For the LORD God is a sun and shield;
    the LORD bestows favor and honor;
no good thing does he withhold
    from those whose walk is blameless.

Psalm 84:10–11

An honest answer
    is like a kiss on the lips.

Proverbs 24:26

Righteousness guards the man of integrity.

Proverbs 13:6

The LORD has dealt with me according to my
    righteousness;
    according to the cleanness of my hands he
        has rewarded me.
For I have kept the ways of the LORD;
    I have not done evil by turning from my God.
All his laws are before me;
    I have not turned away from his decrees.
I have been blameless before him
    and have kept myself from sin.
The LORD has rewarded me according to my
    righteousness,
    according to the cleanness of my hands in
        his sight.

Psalm 18:20–24

Who may ascend the hill of the LORD?
    Who may stand in his holy place?
He who has clean hands and a pure heart,
    who does not lift up his soul to an idol
    or swear by what is false.

Psalm 24:3–4

devotional thought
on integrity

Ahab knew Micaiah was a prophet who spoke what God directed, yet he still ignored that divine voice. As for Micaiah, even though he was encouraged to say what the king wanted to hear, he chose to maintain his integrity and speak the truth.

Are you an Ahab? Have you taken a course of action in your life that you know is directly against God's plan? If so, wake up! A life lived contrary to God's will can and probably will leave you endangered and exposed.

Or are you like Micaiah? Have you felt pressure to tell your friends, your family, or your coworkers what they want to hear, even though you sense the right course of action from God's perspective? If so, take heart. Stick to your guns. Your integrity before God is more important than your reputation in the office or at the next family gathering.

promises for life
on leadership

The LORD said to Joshua, "Be strong and courageous, because you will lead these people to inherit the land I swore to their forefathers to give them. Be strong and very courageous. Be careful to obey all the law my servant Moses gave you; do not turn from it to the right or to the left, that you may be successful wherever you go. Do not let this Book of the Law depart from your mouth; meditate on it day and night, so that you may be careful to do everything written in it. Then you will be prosperous and successful. Have I not commanded you? Be strong and courageous. Do not be terrified; do not be discouraged, for the LORD your God will be with you wherever you go."

Joshua 1:6–9

for men

Jesus called [his disciples] together and said, "You know that the rulers of the Gentiles lord it over them, and their high officials exercise authority over them. Not so with you. Instead, whoever wants to become great among you must be your servant, and whoever wants to be first must be your slave—just as the Son of Man did not come to be served, but to serve."

Matthew 20:25–28

"Do you understand what I have done for you?" [Jesus] asked them. "You call me 'Teacher' and 'Lord,' and rightly so, for that is what I am. Now that I, your Lord and Teacher, have washed your feet, you also should wash one another's feet. I have set you an example that you should do as I have done for you."

John 13:12–15

In everything set them an example by doing what is good.

Titus 2:7

promises for life
on leadership

*Since an overseer is entrusted with God's work, he
must be ... hospitable, one who loves what is good,
who is self-controlled, upright, holy and disciplined.
He must hold firmly to the trustworthy message as it
has been taught, so that he can encourage others by
sound doctrine and refute those who oppose it.*

Titus 1:7–9

*If anyone sets his heart on being an overseer, he
desires a noble task. Now the overseer must be above
reproach, the husband of but one wife, temperate,
self-controlled, respectable, hospitable, able to teach,
not given to drunkenness, not violent but gentle, not
quarrelsome, not a lover of money. He must manage
his own family well and see that his children obey
him with proper respect.*

1 Timothy 3:1–4

"I will give you shepherds after my own heart, who will lead you with knowledge and understanding," declares the LORD.

Jeremiah 3:15

Jesus said, "Simon son of John, do you truly love me?" He answered, "Yes, Lord, you know that I love you." Jesus said, "Take care of my sheep."

John 21:16

Solomon answered God, "You have shown great kindness to David my father and have made me king in his place. Now, LORD God, let your promise to my father David be confirmed, for you have made me king over a people who are as numerous as the dust of the earth. Give me wisdom and knowledge, that I may lead this people."

2 Chronicles 1:8–10

Those who are wise will shine like the brightness of the heavens, and those who lead many to righteousness, like the stars for ever and ever.

Daniel 12:3

for men

We have different gifts, according to the grace given us. If a man's gift is prophesying, let him use it in proportion to his faith. If it is serving, let him serve; if it is teaching, let him teach; if it is encouraging, let him encourage; if it is contributing to the needs of others, let him give generously; if it is leadership, let him govern diligently.

Romans 12:6–8

Be shepherds of God's flock that is under your care, serving as overseers—not because you must, but because you are willing, as God wants you to be; not greedy for money, but eager to serve; not lording it over those entrusted to you, but being examples to the flock. And when the Chief Shepherd appears, you will receive the crown of glory that will never fade away.

1 Peter 5:2–4

devotional thought
on leadership

King Asa led Judah back to worshiping the one true God. He changed the course of his own personal life and in the process changed the course of the nation he led.

Perhaps, like Asa, you've inherited patterns that you know don't please God. Perhaps you came from a family that ignored—or even ridiculed—the practice of worship and the presence of God in the family's life. Perhaps abusive behavior and a quick temper are part of your family legacy. Or perhaps unfaithfulness, deception, and greed are family "traditions" that prevent you from becoming the man God wants you to be.

You don't have to continue to practice these negative traditions. You can make different decisions; you can change, with God's help. And the change to your own heart and life can have a long-lasting impact on the lives of those whom you influence on a daily basis.

promises for life
on listening

An angel appeared to Moses in the flames of a burning bush in the desert near Mount Sinai. When he saw this, he was amazed at the sight. As he went over to look more closely, he heard the Lord's voice.

Acts 7:30–31

I saw the glory of the God of Israel coming from the east. His voice was like the roar of rushing waters, and the land was radiant with his glory.

Ezekiel 43:2

God spoke to Israel in a vision at night and said, "Jacob! Jacob!" "Here I am," he replied.

Genesis 46:2

I heard the voice of the Lord saying, "Whom shall I send? And who will go for us?" And I said, "Here am I. Send me!"

Isaiah 6:8

This is what the LORD says, he who made the earth, the LORD who formed it and established it — the LORD is his name: "Call to me and I will answer you and tell you great and unsearchable things you do not know."

Jeremiah 33:2–3

Seek the LORD while he may be found;
   call on him while he is near.

Isaiah 55:6

You will call, and the LORD will answer;
   you will cry for help, and he will say: Here am I.

Isaiah 58:9

Whether you turn to the right or to the left, your ears will hear a voice behind you, saying, "This is the way; walk in it."

Isaiah 30:21

I call on you, O God, for you will answer me;
   give ear to me and hear my prayer.

Psalm 17:6

for men

In the past God spoke to our forefathers through the prophets at many times and in various ways, but in these last days he has spoken to us by his Son, whom he appointed heir of all things, and through whom he made the universe. The Son is the radiance of God's glory and the exact representation of his being.

Hebrews 1:1–3

While [Jesus] was still speaking, a bright cloud enveloped them, and a voice from the cloud said, "This is my Son, whom I love; with him I am well pleased. Listen to him!"

Matthew 17:5

Jesus said, "My sheep listen to my voice; I know them, and they follow me."

John 10:27

Speak, LORD, for your servant is listening.

1 Samuel 3:9

devotional thought
on listening

Ever had a "burning bush" experience? God could be trying to speak to you through almost any situation. Children and spouses, for example, often have penetrating insights into God's direction for our lives. God often speaks to us through the voices of those close to us.

But there are times when God's voice speaks through larger events as well. When one software engineer received a pink slip, he realized it was a burning bush moment. He decided to finally answer a tug on his heart to become a pastor. He sold his home, moved his family to an apartment, and started seminary classes.

Burning bushes show up in many forms, but they all have one critical thing in common: they're life changing. They rarely make life easier—just more meaningful. But like Moses, we have to be willing to stop, tune in to what God is saying, and boldly follow him.

promises for life
on love

Let love and faithfulness never leave you;
    bind them around your neck,
    write them on the tablet of your heart.
Then you will win favor and a good name
    in the sight of God and man.

Proverbs 3:3–4

Clothe yourselves with compassion, kindness, humility, gentleness and patience. Bear with each other and forgive whatever grievances you may have against one another. Forgive as the Lord forgave you. And over all these virtues put on love, which binds them all together in perfect unity.

Colossians 3:12–14

Love is patient, love is kind. It does not envy, it does not boast, it is not proud. It is not rude, it is not self-seeking, it is not easily angered, it keeps no record of wrongs. Love does not delight in evil but rejoices with the truth. It always protects, always trusts, always hopes, always perseveres. Love never fails.

1 Corinthians 13:4–8

The apostle Paul wrote, "I pray that you, being rooted and established in love, may have power, together with all the saints, to grasp how wide and long and high and deep is the love of Christ, and to know this love that surpasses knowledge—that you may be filled to the measure of all the fullness of God."

Ephesians 3:17–19

Christ's love compels us.

2 Corinthians 5:14

Be imitators of God, therefore, as dearly loved children and live a life of love, just as Christ loved us and gave himself up for us as a fragrant offering and sacrifice to God.

Ephesians 5:1–2

We love because [God] first loved us.

1 John 4:19

Dear friends, let us love one another, for love comes from God. Everyone who loves has been born of God and knows God.

1 John 4:7

121

promises for life
on love

The apostle Paul wrote, "If I have a faith that can move mountains, but have not love, I am nothing. If I give all I possess to the poor and surrender my body to the flames, but have not love, I gain nothing."

1 Corinthians 13:2–3

Knowledge puffs up, but love builds up.

1 Corinthians 8:1

Jesus said, "A new command I give you: Love one another. As I have loved you, so you must love one another."

John 13:34

Do everything in love.

1 Corinthians 16:14

God has poured out his love into our hearts by the Holy Spirit, whom he has given us.

Romans 5:5

God is love. Whoever lives in love lives in God, and God in him.

1 John 4:16

The only thing that counts is faith expressing itself through love.

Galatians 5:6

Jesus replied: "'Love the Lord your God with all your heart and with all your soul and with all your mind.' This is the first and greatest commandment. And the second is like it: 'Love your neighbor as yourself.'"

Matthew 22:37–39

Jesus said: "Love your enemies, do good to those who hate you, bless those who curse you, pray for those who mistreat you. If someone strikes you on one cheek, turn to him the other also."

Luke 6:27–29

He who pursues righteousness and love
    finds life, prosperity and honor.

Proverbs 21:21

Above all, love each other deeply, because love covers over a multitude of sins.

1 Peter 4:8

for men

The fruit of the Spirit is love, joy, peace, patience, kindness, goodness, faithfulness, gentleness and self-control.

Galatians 5:22–23

And now these three remain: faith, hope and love. But the greatest of these is love.

1 Corinthians 13:13

Let no debt remain outstanding, except the continuing debt to love one another, for he who loves his fellowman has fulfilled the law. The commandments, "Do not commit adultery," "Do not murder," "Do not steal," "Do not covet," and whatever other commandment there may be, are summed up in this one rule: "Love your neighbor as yourself." Love does no harm to its neighbor. Therefore love is the fulfillment of the law.

Romans 13:8–10

Greater love has no one than this, that he lay down his life for his friends.

John 15:13

devotional thought
on love

No matter what grand things we might accomplish, no matter what fine vision we might believe, no matter what deep and difficult truths we might learn, if we leave out love, it all means nothing.

Without love, we fail. With it, we can't help but succeed.

Does that sound too easy? Well, people who've never tried it might think so. But this love is different from the natural love we've experienced. This kind of love combines virtues such as patience, honesty, forgiveness, trust, and good manners. Further, it rules out self-interested motives.

This kind of love isn't easy at all. Yet it stands as the central characteristic of faith.

Jesus doesn't say that people will recognize us by our knowledge of Scripture or by stands we make against our culture. While those things have their place, Jesus simply says that others will recognize us as belonging to him by our love.

promises for life
on mentors

The glory of young men is their strength,
    gray hair the splendor of the old.

Proverbs 20:29

Encourage the young men to be self-controlled. In everything set them an example by doing what is good. In your teaching show integrity, seriousness and soundness of speech.

Titus 2:6–8

My son, pay attention to what I say;
    listen closely to my words.
Do not let them out of your sight,
    keep them within your heart;
for they are life to those who find them
    and health to a man's whole body.

Proverbs 4:20–22

Let us consider how we may spur one another on toward love and good deeds.

Hebrews 10:24

Set an example for the believers in speech, in life, in love, in faith and in purity.

1 Timothy 4:12

devotional thought
on mentors

Elijah served as Elisha's mentor long before that word was coined. Elijah believed in Elisha and wanted him to succeed as a prophet. Elijah willingly offered himself to Elisha to assure the younger prophet's success. God brought Elijah into Elisha's life to prepare, train, and befriend him for fulfilling the role of prophet to the nation of Israel.

Do you have a spiritual mentor? Mentoring goes well beyond information and activity. It builds on the maturity and integrity of the individuals in the mentoring relationship. Mentoring brings in a level of accountability that fosters growth and helps one stay on the right path. Or perhaps you could consider offering your wisdom to another person who is new to the faith or faltering in his walk with God. Either way, take a moment to consider how mentoring could play a role in your spiritual development.

promises for life
on money

Jesus said, "Do not store up for yourselves treasures on earth, where moth and rust destroy, and where thieves break in and steal. But store up for yourselves treasures in heaven, where moth and rust do not destroy, and where thieves do not break in and steal. For where your treasure is, there your heart will be also."

Matthew 6:19–21

Jesus said, "Whoever can be trusted with very little can also be trusted with much, and whoever is dishonest with very little will also be dishonest with much. So if you have not been trustworthy in handling worldly wealth, who will trust you with true riches?"

Luke 16:10–11

Jesus said, "Give, and it will be given to you. A good measure, pressed down, shaken together and running over, will be poured into your lap. For with the measure you use, it will be measured to you."

Luke 6:38

Honor the LORD with your wealth,
> with the firstfruits of all your crops;
then your barns will be filled to overflowing,
> and your vats will brim over with new wine.

Proverbs 3:9–10

Keep your lives free from the love of money and be content with what you have.

Hebrews 13:5

As he looked up, Jesus saw the rich putting their gifts into the temple treasury. He also saw a poor widow put in two very small copper coins. "I tell you the truth," he said, "this poor widow has put in more than all the others. All these people gave their gifts out of their wealth; but she out of her poverty put in all she had to live on."

Luke 21:1–4

promises for life
on money

Godliness with contentment is great gain. For we brought nothing into the world, and we can take nothing out of it. But if we have food and clothing, we will be content with that. People who want to get rich fall into temptation and a trap and into many foolish and harmful desires that plunge men into ruin and destruction. For the love of money is a root of all kinds of evil. Some people, eager for money, have wandered from the faith and pierced themselves with many griefs.

1 Timothy 6:6–10

Jesus said, "When you give to the needy, do not let your left hand know what your right hand is doing, so that your giving may be in secret. Then your Father, who sees what is done in secret, will reward you."

Matthew 6:3–4

The house of the righteous contains great treasure.

Proverbs 15:6

for men

You may say to yourself, "My power and the strength of my hands have produced this wealth for me." But remember the LORD your God, for it is he who gives you the ability to produce wealth.

Deuteronomy 8:17–18

The blessing of the LORD brings wealth,
    and he adds no trouble to it.

Proverbs 10:22

Bring the whole tithe into the storehouse, that there may be food in my house. Test me in this," says the LORD Almighty, "and see if I will not throw open the floodgates of heaven and pour out so much blessing that you will not have room enough for it."

Malachi 3:10

One man pretends to be rich, yet has nothing;
    another pretends to be poor, yet has
        great wealth.

Proverbs 13:7

A good man leaves an inheritance for his children's children.

Proverbs 13:22

Do not wear yourself out to get rich;
　　have the wisdom to show restraint.
Cast but a glance at riches, and they are gone,
　　for they will surely sprout wings
　　and fly off to the sky like an eagle.

Proverbs 23:4–5

Jesus said, "No one can serve two masters. Either
he will hate the one and love the other, or he will be
devoted to the one and despise the other. You cannot
serve both God and Money."

Matthew 6:24

Dishonest money dwindles away,
　　but he who gathers money little by little makes
　　　　it grow.

Proverbs 13:11

Whoever sows sparingly will also reap sparingly, and
whoever sows generously will also reap generously.
Each man should give what he has decided in his
heart to give, not reluctantly or under compulsion, for
God loves a cheerful giver.

2 Corinthians 9:6–7

devotional thought

on money

The young son eagerly bounces over to Dad with a poorly but carefully wrapped present—jumping up and down, eyes shining, unable to contain his excitement.

Maybe this child's eagerness comes close to the idea of the "cheerful giving" God desires of us. The apostle Paul offers good reasons for giving generously to the Lord's work: God promises a generous return; our giving prompts others to praise God; our gifts cause others to pray for us.

Sure, we appreciate all these benefits. Yet, underlying each one is the fact that we give because we want to! We give generously because we love the Lord. Our gift causes a "cheerfulness" within that the world can't begin to understand.

God loves to see our open hands. He delights in our understanding that he loves us, provides for us and invites us to participate in his work by giving back to him financially.

promises for life
on obedience

Jesus said, "Everyone who hears these words of mine and puts them into practice is like a wise man who built his house on the rock. The rain came down, the streams rose, and the winds blew and beat against that house; yet it did not fall, because it had its foundation on the rock."

Matthew 7:24–25

I will hasten and not delay
    to obey your commands, [O Lᴏʀᴅ].

Psalm 119:60

Noah did everything just as God commanded him.

Genesis 6:22

Do not merely listen to the word, and so deceive yourselves. Do what it says.

James 1:22

To obey is better than sacrifice.

1 Samuel 15:22

"Obey me, and I will be your God and you will be my people. Walk in all the ways I command you, that it may go well with you," declares the Lᴏʀᴅ.

Jeremiah 7:23

devotional thought
on obedience

Imagine what might have happened if Abraham had set out on his own way instead of taking the journey God set before him. Ultimately, Abraham willingly left behind everything and everyone he knew to follow God's will. Yet as a direct result of his obedience, Abraham experienced God's blessings—and the rewards were greater than he could ever have imagined.

God desires the same for you. When you begin a relationship with him, he calls you to leave behind what's comfortable and familiar to set out on a journey filled with wonder, blessing, and the promise of a new life. On your journey to obedience, you'll leave behind old habits, old attitudes, old sins, and old ways of thinking. But the blessing that awaits is greater than you can ever imagine.

When you allow him to guide you, God offers a full and satisfying journey through life and a home for eternity.

promises for life
on possessions

Every good and perfect gift is from above, coming down from the Father of the heavenly lights.

James 1:17

When God gives any man wealth and possessions, and enables him to enjoy them, to accept his lot and be happy in his work—this is a gift of God.

Ecclesiastes 5:19

Jesus said, "Be on your guard against all kinds of greed; a man's life does not consist in the abundance of his possessions."

Luke 12:15

Jesus said, "If you want to be perfect, go, sell your possessions and give to the poor, and you will have treasure in heaven. Then come, follow me."

Matthew 19:21

All the believers were together and had everything in common. Selling their possessions and goods, they gave to anyone as he had need.

Acts 2:44–45

devotional thought
on possessions

Imagine being put in Abraham's position; being asked to sacrifice your only son; wondering why God would ask for such a devastating act of obedience. What would you do?

Of course, we know the end of the story. Isaac was never in danger. But Abraham was. He could have clung to his son like a jeweled crown, a prized possession. God tested Abraham's heart to clarify who came first in his life. The answer came back clearly: "You do, God."

We don't possess what we have in this life: our jobs, our homes, our toys. Similarly, our children, families, and friends are entrusted to us for a time, and it is up to us to influence them toward following God while we have the opportunity. We need to follow Abraham's example and hold our possessions and relationships loosely, to be used as God intends.

promises for life
on prayer

Jesus often withdrew to lonely places and prayed.

Luke 5:16

I am a man of prayer.

Psalm 109:4

Jesus replied, "If you believe, you will receive whatever you ask for in prayer."

Matthew 21:22

Jesus said, "Ask and it will be given to you; seek and you will find; knock and the door will be opened to you. For everyone who asks receives; he who seeks finds and to him who knocks, the door will be opened."

Luke 11:9–10

They devoted themselves to the apostles' teaching and to the fellowship, to the breaking of bread and to prayer.

Acts 2:42

Be joyful always; pray continually; give thanks in all circumstances, for this is God's will for you in Christ Jesus.

1 Thessalonians 5:16–18

God said, "If my people, who are called by my name, will humble themselves and pray and seek my face and turn from their wicked ways, then will I hear from heaven and will forgive their sin and will heal their land."

2 Chronicles 7:14

Jesus told his disciples a parable to show them that they should always pray and not give up.

Luke 18:1

As the deer pants for streams of water,
    so my soul pants for you, O God.
My soul thirsts for God, for the living God.
    When can I go and meet with God?

Psalm 42:1–2

Be joyful in hope, patient in affliction, faithful in prayer.

Romans 12:12

Pray in the Spirit on all occasions with all kinds of prayers and requests. With this in mind, be alert and always keep on praying for all the saints.

Ephesians 6:18

promises for life
on prayer

The apostle Paul wrote, "I want men everywhere to lift up holy hands in prayer."

1 Timothy 2:8

*The eyes of the Lord are on the righteous
    and his ears are attentive to their prayer.*

1 Peter 3:12

While I was still in prayer, Gabriel, the man I had seen in the earlier vision, came to me in swift flight about the time of the evening sacrifice. He instructed me and said to me, "Daniel, I have now come to give you insight and understanding. As soon as you began to pray, an answer was given, which I have come to tell you, for you are highly esteemed."

Daniel 9:21–23

The prayer of a righteous man is powerful and effective.

James 5:16

"Before they call I will answer;
    while they are still speaking I will hear,"
        says the LORD.

Isaiah 65:24

Jesus said, "When you pray, go into your room, close the door and pray to your Father, who is unseen. Then your Father, who sees what is done in secret, will reward you."

Matthew 6:6

Jesus said, "When you stand praying, if you hold anything against anyone, forgive him, so that your Father in heaven may forgive you your sins."

Mark 11:25

The Spirit helps us in our weakness. We do not know what we ought to pray for, but the Spirit himself intercedes for us with groans that words cannot express. And he who searches our hearts knows the mind of the Spirit, because the Spirit intercedes for the saints in accordance with God's will.

Romans 8:26–27

Christ Jesus, who died—more than that, who was raised to life—is at the right hand of God and is also interceding for us.

Romans 8:34

The apostle Paul wrote, "I urge you, brothers, by our Lord Jesus Christ and by the love of the Spirit, to join me in my struggle by praying to God for me."

Romans 15:30

Jesus said, "This, then, is how you should pray:
    'Our Father in heaven,
    hallowed be your name,
    your kingdom come,
    your will be done
        on earth as it is in heaven.
    Give us today our daily bread.
    Forgive us our debts,
        as we also have forgiven our debtors.
    And lead us not into temptation,
        but deliver us from the evil one.'"

Matthew 6:9–13

Do not be anxious about anything, but in everything, by prayer and petition, with thanksgiving, present your requests to God. And the peace of God, which transcends all understanding, will guard your hearts and your minds in Christ Jesus.

Philippians 4:6–7

devotional thought
on prayer

When a tragic event occurs in our lives, most of us have the overwhelming desire to make something happen. Fix it. Take action, even if it's wrong. That's a typical guy's first response; it's the way most of us are hardwired.

How often do we act first and then pray? We ask God to bless what we're doing already, rather than seeking him first for direction. Our pride and feelings of self-sufficiency can keep us from prayer. Like a laser-guided missile, nothing gets in our way until we follow a straight path directly to where we want to go, regardless of the repercussions of our actions.

Instead, we need to realize just how needy we are and how amazingly generous God is. Humility and admitting we need God's sufficiency will drive us to prayer. As the old saying goes, the best way to begin a journey is on your knees.

promises for life
on purpose

I cry out to God Most High,
to God, who fulfills his purpose for me.

Psalm 57:2

*"I know the plans I have for you," declares the LORD,
"plans to prosper you and not to harm you, plans to
give you hope and a future."*

Jeremiah 29:11

All the days ordained for me
were written in your book, [O LORD,]
before one of them came to be.

Psalm 139:16

The word of the LORD came to me, saying,
"Before I formed you in the womb I knew you,
before you were born I set you apart."

Jeremiah 1:4–5

*In [Christ] we were also chosen, having been
predestined according to the plan of God who works
out everything in conformity with the purpose of
his will.*

Ephesians 1:11

We are God's workmanship, created in Christ Jesus to do good works, which God prepared in advance for us to do.

Ephesians 2:10

The LORD will fulfill his purpose for me.

Psalm 138:8

Mordecai said to Esther, "Who knows but that you have come to royal position for such a time as this?"

Esther 4:12–14

In all things God works for the good of those who love him, who have been called according to his purpose.

Romans 8:28

God ... has saved us and called us to a holy life—not because of anything we have done but because of his own purpose and grace.

2 Timothy 1:8–9

It is God who works in you to will and to act according to his good purpose.

Philippians 2:13

for men

Do not conform any longer to the pattern of this world, but be transformed by the renewing of your mind. Then you will be able to test and approve what God's will is—his good, pleasing and perfect will.

Romans 12:2

If the whole body were an eye, where would the sense of hearing be? If the whole body were an ear, where would the sense of smell be? But in fact God has arranged the parts in the body, every one of them, just as he wanted them to be…. You are the body of Christ, and each one of you is a part of it.

1 Corinthians 12:17–18, 27

Neither he who plants nor he who waters is anything, but only God, who makes things grow. The man who plants and the man who waters have one purpose, and each will be rewarded according to his own labor. For we are God's fellow workers.

1 Corinthians 3:7–9

He who began a good work in you will carry it on to completion.

Philippians 1:6

devotional thought

on purpose

Do you ever feel like duct tape? Do you feel like you can do almost anything, but you don't know what God really wants you to do? Paul explains that God created each of us for a specific role and purpose within the body of Christ. He also supplies each of us with unique gifts and talents.

Think about how you impact the lives of others, and you may begin to see a pattern emerging. Perhaps God is using you—even temporarily—to fulfill his plans and purposes in the lives of your friends, family, or coworkers.

Ask, "How can I help?" "Who does God want me to serve?" "What needs can I address?" God will start to use you to make smaller repairs in the lives of others, as in fact he may already be doing. You may just find out that you are on track to discover your true calling.

promises for life
on righteous living

Jesus said,
> "Blessed are the pure in heart,
>> for they will see God."

Matthew 5:8

The grace of God that brings salvation has appeared to all men. It teaches us to say "No" to ungodliness and worldly passions, and to live self-controlled, upright and godly lives in this present age, while we wait for the blessed hope — the glorious appearing of our great God and Savior, Jesus Christ, who gave himself for us to redeem us from all wickedness and to purify for himself a people that are his very own, eager to do what is good.

Titus 2:11–14

He who pursues righteousness and love
> finds life, prosperity and honor.

Proverbs 21:21

Live as free men, but do not use your freedom as a cover-up for evil; live as servants of God.

1 Peter 2:16

The LORD ... hears the prayer of the righteous.

Proverbs 15:29

*What does the LORD your God ask of you but to fear
the LORD your God, to walk in all his ways, to love
him, to serve the LORD your God with all your heart
and with all your soul, and to observe the LORD's
commands and decrees that I am giving you today for
your own good?*

Deuteronomy 10:12–13

He has showed you, O man, what is good.
      And what does the LORD require of you?
To act justly and to love mercy
      and to walk humbly with your God.

Micah 6:8

David told Solomon, "Be strong, show yourself
a man, and observe what the LORD your God
requires: Walk in his ways, and keep his decrees and
commands, his laws and requirements, as written in
the Law of Moses, so that you may prosper in all you
do and wherever you go."

1 Kings 2:2–3

for men

"Suppose there is a righteous man
    who does what is just and right.
He does not oppress anyone,
    but returns what he took in pledge for a loan.
He does not commit robbery
    but gives his food to the hungry
    and provides clothing for the naked.
He does not lend at usury
    or take excessive interest.
He withholds his hand from doing wrong
    and judges fairly between man and man.
He follows my decrees
    and faithfully keeps my laws.
That man is righteous;
    he will surely live,"
                declares the Sovereign LORD.

Ezekiel 18:5, 7 – 9

Surely God is good to Israel,
    to those who are pure in heart.

Psalm 73:1

devotional thought
on righteous living

Just as brand names like Kleenex lose their distinction, so do words we use every day. That was the case with the rich young man who asked Jesus about what "good thing" he could do to gain eternal life (Matthew 19:16–21). Jesus questioned why the young man used the word *good*.

Then the Lord delivered the laundry list. In essence, he said that the only thing good enough to earn eternal life involves living a perfect, obedient, and selfless life—something that no man can do.

However, we often overlook the two simple words that followed Jesus' impossible-to-attain list.

Jesus' simple two-word directive is filled with deep and complex meaning. With those words, he calls us to go with him on his mission, to tag along on the journey through life. We can't really accomplish any "good" on our own. We can only answer yes when Jesus says, "Follow me."

promises for life
on security

[The LORD] will not let your foot slip—
  he who watches over you will not slumber;
indeed, he who watches over Israel
  will neither slumber nor sleep.

Psalm 121:3–4

Jesus said, "Everyone who hears these words of mine and puts them into practice is like a wise man who built his house on the rock. The rain came down, the streams rose, and the winds blew and beat against that house; yet it did not fall, because it had its foundation on the rock."

Matthew 7:24–25

I am always with you, O LORD;
  you hold me by my right hand.
You guide me with your counsel,
  and afterward you will take me into glory.

Psalm 73:23–24

L<small>ORD</small>, you have assigned me my portion and my cup;
   you have made my lot secure.
The boundary lines have fallen for me in pleasant
                  places;
      surely I have a delightful inheritance.

Psalm 16:5–6

[The L<small>ORD</small>] is a shield
   for all who take refuge in him.
For who is God besides the L<small>ORD</small>?
   And who is the Rock except our God?

2 Samuel 22:31–32

I will say of the L<small>ORD</small>, "He is my refuge and
               my fortress,
   my God, in whom I trust."

Psalm 91:2

There is surely a future hope for you,
   and your hope will not be cut off.

Proverbs 23:18

promises for life
on security

I will praise the Lord, who counsels me;
    even at night my heart instructs me.
I have set the Lord always before me.
    Because he is at my right hand,
    I will not be shaken.

Psalm 16:7–8

The path of the righteous is level;
    O upright One, you make the way of
        the righteous smooth.

Isaiah 26:7

Let the beloved of the Lord rest secure in him,
    for he shields him all day long,
    and the one the Lord loves rests between
        his shoulders.

Deuteronomy 33:12

"Even to your old age and gray hairs
    I am he, I am he who will sustain you.
I have made you and I will carry you;
    I will sustain you and I will rescue you,"
        declares the Lord.

Isaiah 46:4

Because God wanted to make the unchanging nature of his purpose very clear to the heirs of what was promised, he confirmed it with an oath. God did this so that ... we who have fled to take hold of the hope offered to us may be greatly encouraged. We have this hope as an anchor for the soul, firm and secure.

Hebrews 6:17–19

It is God who arms me with strength
    and makes my way perfect.
He makes my feet like the feet of a deer;
    he enables me to stand on the heights.
He trains my hands for battle;
    my arms can bend a bow of bronze.
You give me your shield of victory;
    you stoop down to make me great.
You broaden the path beneath me,
    so that my ankles do not turn.

2 Samuel 22:33–37

for men

The LORD is my rock, my fortress and my deliverer;
   my God is my rock, in whom I take refuge.
He is my shield and the horn of my salvation,
   my stronghold.

Psalm 18:2

[The LORD] shielded him and cared for him;
   he guarded him as the apple of his eye,
like an eagle that stirs up its nest
   and hovers over its young,
that spreads its wings to catch them
   and carries them on its pinions.

Deuteronomy 32:10 – 11

My heart is glad and my tongue rejoices;
   my body also will rest secure,
because you will not abandon me to the grave,
   nor will you let your Holy One see decay.
You have made known to me the path of life;
   you will fill me with joy in your presence,
   with eternal pleasures at your right hand.

Psalm 16:9 – 11

devotional thought
on security

The composer of Psalm 91 clearly experienced a deep relationship with God. He wrote this psalm to assure others that those who trust in God can expect security. Such a relationship takes discipline—relying on God, meditating on his Word, believing in God's character and promises, praying regularly.

How's your relationship with God? Maybe you've always harbored the feeling that relying on God's strength means admitting your own weaknesses. Maybe a personal relationship sounds too "emotional" for you. Or maybe you feel you're just too busy earning a living and taking care of your family to invest the time to deepen your relationship with God.

Look at it this way: disciplines like trusting, meditating, praying and accepting God's control over your life constitute a battle plan. Carrying out the strategy takes time and resolve. But in return, these disciplines strengthen your spiritual muscles for any challenges that may lie ahead.

promises for life
on serving

Jesus said, "Whoever wants to become great among
you must be your servant, and whoever wants to be
first must be your slave—just as the Son of Man did
not come to be served, but to serve, and to give his life
as a ransom for many."

Matthew 20:26–28

Your attitude should be the same as that of
Christ Jesus:
Who, being in very nature God,
    did not consider equality with God something
        to be grasped,
but made himself nothing,
    taking the very nature of a servant.

Philippians 2:5–7

[Jesus] now showed them the full extent of his love....
He got up from the meal, took off his outer clothing,
and wrapped a towel around his waist. After that,
he poured water into a basin and began to wash his
disciples' feet, drying them with the towel that was
wrapped around him.

John 13:1, 4–5

Each one should use whatever gift he has received to serve others, faithfully administering God's grace in its various forms. If anyone speaks, he should do it as one speaking the very words of God. If anyone serves, he should do it with the strength God provides, so that in all things God may be praised through Jesus Christ.

1 Peter 4:10–11

You, my brothers, were called to be free. But do not use your freedom to indulge the sinful nature; rather, serve one another in love.

Galatians 5:13

There are different kinds of gifts, but the same Spirit. There are different kinds of service, but the same Lord. There are different kinds of working, but the same God works all of them in all men.

1 Corinthians 12:4–6

Religion that God our Father accepts as pure and faultless is this: to look after orphans and widows in their distress.

James 1:27

What good is it, my brothers, if a man claims to have faith but has no deeds? Can such faith save him? Suppose a brother or sister is without clothes and daily food. If one of you says to him, "Go, I wish you well; keep warm and well fed," but does nothing about his physical needs, what good is it? In the same way, faith by itself, if it is not accompanied by action, is dead. But someone will say, "You have faith; I have deeds." Show me your faith without deeds, and I will show you my faith by what I do.

James 2:14–18

Good deeds are obvious, and even those that are not cannot be hidden.

1 Timothy 5:25

devotional thought
on serving

Long before Jesus was born, Isaiah wrote that the coming Messiah would be a servant. And during his ministry on earth, Jesus identified himself as a servant.

Service characterized Jesus' ministry from beginning to end. He healed the sick and fed the hungry. He gave comfort to those who grieved. He put himself last and served others first. People clamored to be close to him, to touch him, to hear his words and to possibly be healed. His service attracted others because it was so countercultural. And Jesus' ultimate act of service meant giving his life as a sacrifice for our sins.

True service involves setting your own interests and perspectives aside and looking to handle the needs of others. When you commit to this kind of activity, others will be attracted to you because of your selfless quality—the same quality that marked the life of Jesus.

promises for life
on spiritual growth

Speaking the truth in love, we will in all things grow up into him who is the Head, that is, Christ. From him the whole body, joined and held together by every supporting ligament, grows and builds itself up in love, as each part does its work.

Ephesians 4:15–16

Jesus told this parable: "A farmer went out to sow his seed. As he was scattering the seed, some fell along the path; it was trampled on, and the birds of the air ate it up. Some fell on rock, and when it came up, the plants withered because they had no moisture. Other seed fell among thorns, which grew up with it and choked the plants. Still other seed fell on good soil. It came up and yielded a crop, a hundred times more than was sown."

Luke 8:4–7

Jesus said, "This is the meaning of the parable: The seed is the word of God. Those along the path are the ones who hear, and then the devil comes and takes away the word from their hearts, so that they may not believe and be saved. Those on the rock are the ones who receive the word with joy when they hear it, but they have no root. They believe for a while, but in the time of testing they fall away. The seed that fell among thorns stands for those who hear, but as they go on their way they are choked by life's worries, riches and pleasures, and they do not mature. But the seed on good soil stands for those with a noble and good heart, who hear the word, retain it, and by persevering produce a crop."

Luke 8:11 – 15

The apostle Paul wrote, "Epaphras … is always wrestling in prayer for you, that you may stand firm in all the will of God, mature and fully assured."

Colossians 4:12

promises for life
on spiritual growth

O LORD, you are our Father.
>   We are the clay, you are the potter;
>   we are all the work of your hand.

Isaiah 64:8

*Anyone who lives on milk, being still an infant, is not
acquainted with the teaching about righteousness.
But solid food is for the mature, who by constant use
have trained themselves to distinguish good from evil.
Therefore let us leave the elementary teachings about
Christ and go on to maturity.*

Hebrews 5:13 – 6:1

*Just as you received Christ Jesus as Lord, continue
to live in him, rooted and built up in him,
strengthened in the faith as you were taught, and
overflowing with thankfulness.*

Colossians 2:6 – 7

*Consider it pure joy, my brothers, whenever you
face trials of many kinds, because you know that
the testing of your faith develops perseverance.
Perseverance must finish its work so that you may be
mature and complete, not lacking anything.*

James 1:2–4

*The apostle Paul wrote, "I pray that out of God's
glorious riches he may strengthen you with power
through his Spirit in your inner being, so that Christ
may dwell in your hearts through faith. And I pray
that you, being rooted and established in love, may
have power, together with all the saints, to grasp
how wide and long and high and deep is the love
of Christ, and to know this love that surpasses
knowledge — that you may be filled to the measure of
all the fullness of God."*

Ephesians 3:16–19

for men

You, O God, tested us;
  you refined us like silver.

Psalm 66:10

*The apostle Paul wrote, "Whatever was to my profit
I now consider loss for the sake of Christ. What is
more, I consider everything a loss compared to the
surpassing greatness of knowing Christ Jesus my
Lord, for whose sake I have lost all things. I consider
them rubbish, that I may gain Christ and be found
in him, not having a righteousness of my own that
comes from the law, but that which is through faith
in Christ — the righteousness that comes from God
and is by faith. I want to know Christ and the power
of his resurrection and the fellowship of sharing in
his sufferings, becoming like him in his death, and so,
somehow, to attain to the resurrection from the dead."*

Philippians 3:7–11

devotional thought
on spiritual growth

When the risen Christ looked at Paul's resume, the apostle realized that his own qualifications were worthless. If his credentials and achievements fell into the street, someone would come along and shovel them up. "Rubbish," Paul called them (Philippians 3:8).

If Paul ever agonized over the worthlessness of his earlier life, he apparently moved past those thoughts quickly. He leaves it all behind and presses on.

As we move toward Christian maturity, our spiritual resume becomes shorter, not longer. The neatly bulleted list of our youth might contain a fair number of items: decision, total commitment, impeccable doctrine, wholesome lifestyle, self-confidence, unshakeable optimism. Of course, these represent fine qualities. But as life goes on, we increasingly realize that we have no reason to boast in our spiritual accomplishments. The bullets fade from our resumes as Christ and the power of his resurrection take their place.

promises for life
on strength

Be strong in the Lord and in his mighty power.

Ephesians 6:10

[Abraham] did not waver through unbelief regarding the promise of God, but was strengthened in his faith and gave glory to God, being fully persuaded that God had power to do what he had promised.

Romans 4:20–21

The LORD gives strength to his people.

Psalm 29:11

No king is saved by the size of his army;
    no warrior escapes by his great strength.
A horse is a vain hope for deliverance;
    despite all its great strength it cannot save.
But the eyes of the LORD are on those who fear him,
    on those whose hope is in his unfailing love.

Psalm 33:16–18

The LORD is my strength and my song;
    he has become my salvation.

Exodus 15:2

You do not lack any spiritual gift as you eagerly wait for our Lord Jesus Christ to be revealed. He will keep you strong to the end, so that you will be blameless on the day of our Lord Jesus Christ.

1 Corinthians 1:7–8

The LORD is the everlasting God,
    the Creator of the ends of the earth.
He will not grow tired or weary,
    and his understanding no one can fathom.
He gives strength to the weary
    and increases the power of the weak.
Even youths grow tired and weary,
    and young men stumble and fall;
but those who hope in the LORD
    will renew their strength.
They will soar on wings like eagles;
    they will run and not grow weary,
    they will walk and not be faint.

Isaiah 40:28–31

I can do everything through him who gives me strength.

Philippians 4:13

for men

[The Lord] said to me, "My grace is sufficient for you, for my power is made perfect in weakness." Therefore I will boast all the more gladly about my weaknesses, so that Christ's power may rest on me. That is why, for Christ's sake, I delight in weaknesses, in insults, in hardships, in persecutions, in difficulties. For when I am weak, then I am strong.

2 Corinthians 12:9–10

Lift up your heads, O you gates;
    be lifted up, you ancient doors,
      that the King of glory may come in.
Who is this King of glory?
    The LORD strong and mighty,
      the LORD mighty in battle.
Lift up your heads, O you gates;
    lift them up, you ancient doors,
      that the King of glory may come in.
Who is he, this King of glory?
    The LORD Almighty—
      he is the King of glory.

Psalm 24:7–10

devotional thought
on strength

David's men returned home to find their town on fire and their families gone— kidnapped by raiders. Understandably, the men were close to turning on David for getting them into this mess.

How did David handle it? "David found strength in the LORD his God" (1 Samuel 30:6).

David tapped into God's strength just as he always did—in ways available to us. He prayed to God in the morning (see Psalm 5:3). He poured out his complaints to God (see Psalm 62:8). He meditated on the beauty and mercy of God (see Psalm 27:4, 7). With David's renewed strength, he rallied his men. They overtook the raiders and fought them for twenty-four hours. David and his men returned victorious with their families, their possessions, and all that the raiders had plundered from elsewhere.

God still makes his strength available when we look to him. With his strength we can overcome the worst times.

promises for life
on suffering

[Jesus] was despised and rejected by men,
a man of sorrows, and familiar with suffering.

Isaiah 53:3

Now for a little while you may have had to suffer grief in all kinds of trials. These have come so that your faith — of greater worth than gold, which perishes even though refined by fire — may be proved genuine and may result in praise, glory and honor when Jesus Christ is revealed.

1 Peter 1:6–7

There should be no division in the body [of Christ], but ... its parts should have equal concern for each other. If one part suffers, every part suffers with it; if one part is honored, every part rejoices with it.

1 Corinthians 12:25–26

We consider blessed those who have persevered. You have heard of Job's perseverance and have seen what the Lord finally brought about. The Lord is full of compassion and mercy.

James 5:11

We are hard pressed on every side, but not crushed; perplexed, but not in despair; persecuted, but not abandoned; struck down, but not destroyed.

2 Corinthians 4:8–9

Blessed is the man who perseveres under trial, because when he has stood the test, he will receive the crown of life that God has promised to those who love him.

James 1:12

Jesus said,
"Blessed are those who are persecuted
            because of righteousness,
    for theirs is the kingdom of heaven."

Matthew 5:10

We rejoice in the hope of the glory of God. Not only so, but we also rejoice in our sufferings, because we know that suffering produces perseverance; perseverance, character; and character, hope. And hope does not disappoint us, because God has poured out his love into our hearts by the Holy Spirit, whom he has given us.

Romans 5:2–5

on suffering

Remember your word to your servant, [O LORD,]
    for you have given me hope.
My comfort in my suffering is this:
    Your promise preserves my life.

Psalm 119:49–50

*Jesus said, "Blessed are you when people insult you,
persecute you and falsely say all kinds of evil against
you because of me. Rejoice and be glad, because
great is your reward in heaven, for in the same way
they persecuted the prophets who were before you."*

Matthew 5:11–12

*If you are insulted because of the name of Christ,
you are blessed, for the Spirit of glory and of God
rests on you.*

1 Peter 4:14

*Blessed is the man who perseveres under trial,
because when he has stood the test, he will receive
the crown of life that God has promised to those who
love him.*

James 1:12

Jesus said, "If they persecuted me, they will persecute
you also."

John 15:20

If you suffer as a Christian, do not be ashamed, but
praise God that you bear that name.

1 Peter 4:16

It has been granted to you on behalf of Christ not
only to believe on him, but also to suffer for him.

Philippians 1:29

Everyone who wants to live a godly life in Christ Jesus
will be persecuted.

2 Timothy 3:12

Remember Jesus Christ, raised from the dead,
descended from David. This is my gospel, for which I
am suffering even to the point of being chained like a
criminal. But God's word is not chained. Therefore I
endure everything for the sake of the elect, that they
too may obtain the salvation that is in Christ Jesus,
with eternal glory.

2 Timothy 2:8–10

The apostles left the Sanhedrin, rejoicing because they had been counted worthy of suffering disgrace for the Name. Day after day, in the temple courts and from house to house, they never stopped teaching and proclaiming the good news that Jesus is the Christ.

Acts 5:41–42

Those who suffer according to God's will should commit themselves to their faithful Creator and continue to do good.

1 Peter 4:19

Bless those who persecute you; bless and do not curse.

Romans 12:14

We do not lose heart. Though outwardly we are wasting away, yet inwardly we are being renewed day by day. For our light and momentary troubles are achieving for us an eternal glory that far outweighs them all. So we fix our eyes not on what is seen, but on what is unseen. For what is seen is temporary, but what is unseen is eternal.

2 Corinthians 4:16–18

devotional thought
on suffering

Christians find comfort in the midst of painful and trying circumstances through a knowledge of the God who made us and cares for each one of us. And quite often, believers who have been through difficult situations find themselves better equipped to minister to others going through similar issues. When hurting or angry people ask, "Where is God?" they need human spotlights—Christians who illuminate God's actions in dark times. Men and women of faith who help hurting people work through their pain. This is how God delivers his comfort through the darkest times in our lives—through the indwelling of his Holy Spirit in the lives of his people, reaching out to help those in turmoil.

We can demonstrate God's presence in the world by reaching out to hurting people. When they ask, "Where was God ..." we can answer, "God is here, working through me."

promises for life
on temptation

The devil took [Jesus] to a very high mountain and showed him all the kingdoms of the world and their splendor. "All this I will give you," he said, "if you will bow down and worship me." Jesus said to him, "Away from me, Satan! For it is written: 'Worship the Lord your God, and serve him only.'" Then the devil left him, and angels came and attended him.

Matthew 4:8–11

Because he himself suffered when he was tempted, [Jesus] is able to help those who are being tempted.

Hebrews 2:18

There is no truth in [the devil]. When he lies, he speaks his native language, for he is a liar and the father of lies.

John 8:44

Be self-controlled and alert. Your enemy the devil prowls around like a roaring lion looking for someone to devour. Resist him, standing firm in the faith.

1 Peter 5:8–9

Since we have a great high priest who has gone through the heavens, Jesus the Son of God, let us hold firmly to the faith we profess. For we do not have a high priest who is unable to sympathize with our weaknesses, but we have one who has been tempted in every way, just as we are—yet was without sin. Let us then approach the throne of grace with confidence, so that we may receive mercy and find grace to help us in our time of need.

Hebrews 4:14–16

Jesus prayed,
"Lead us not into temptation, heavenly Father,
    but deliver us from the evil one."

Matthew 6:13

Jesus said, "Watch and pray so that you will not fall into temptation. The spirit is willing, but the body is weak."

Matthew 26:41

If you think you are standing firm, be careful that you don't fall!

1 Corinthians 10:12

When tempted, no one should say, "God is tempting me." For God cannot be tempted by evil, nor does he tempt anyone; but each one is tempted when, by his own evil desire, he is dragged away and enticed. Then, after desire has conceived, it gives birth to sin; and sin, when it is full-grown, gives birth to death.

James 1:13 – 15

Then the LORD said to Cain, "If you do not do what is right, sin is crouching at your door; it desires to have you, but you must master it."

Genesis 4:7

No temptation has seized you except what is common to man. And God is faithful; he will not let you be tempted beyond what you can bear. But when you are tempted, he will also provide a way out so that you can stand up under it.

1 Corinthians 10:13

devotional thought
on temptation

When Hernando Cortez, the great Spanish explorer, arrived by ship on the beach at Vera Cruz, Mexico, in 1519, he faced a daunting challenge—conquering the barbaric Aztecs. How could the explorer motivate his men to be brave? How could he avoid insurrection?

The action Cortez took was staggering. He sunk the ships, leaving his men with no way to return to Spain. Only two choices remained—be victorious or die.

Today we wrestle with materialism, greed, pornography, and sexual immorality. How do we overcome these enemies? We first need to renew our commitment to God. But we can also sink the ships. We can destroy our tendency toward materialism by simplifying life and eliminating big-boy toys. We can ask God to give us a different attitude about money and wealth. We can remove the visible temptations that tempt us with different sexual sins.

What ships do you need to sink?

promises for life
on trust

*When the Israelites saw the great power the L*ORD *displayed against the Egyptians, the people feared the* L*ORD and put their trust in him.*

Exodus 14:31

Trust in the LORD with all your heart
    and lean not on your own understanding;
in all your ways acknowledge him,
    and he will make your paths straight.

Proverbs 3:5–6

The LORD says,
"I am the LORD your God,
    who teaches you what is best for you,
    who directs you in the way you should go."

Isaiah 48:17

[God] answered their prayers, because they trusted in him.

1 Chronicles 5:20

Trust in the LORD and do good;
    dwell in the land and enjoy safe pasture.
Delight yourself in the LORD
    and he will give you the desires of your heart.

Psalm 37:3–4

Those who know your name will trust in you,
> for you, LORD, have never forsaken those who
> > seek you.

Psalm 9:10

Blessed is the man
> who makes the LORD his trust.

Psalm 40:4

Let the morning bring me word of your unfailing
> love, [O LORD,]
> for I have put my trust in you.
Show me the way I should go,
> for to you I lift up my soul.

Psalm 143:8

One thing God has spoken,
> two things have I heard:
that you, O God, are strong,
> and that you, O Lord, are loving.

Psalm 62:11–12

*Jesus said, "Do not let your hearts be troubled.
Trust in God; trust also in me."*

John 14:1

for men

Some trust in chariots and some in horses,
    but we trust in the name of the LORD our God.
They are brought to their knees and fall,
    but we rise up and stand firm.

Psalm 20:7–8

*If you confess with your mouth, "Jesus is Lord," and
believe in your heart that God raised him from the
dead, you will be saved. For it is with your heart
that you believe and are justified, and it is with
your mouth that you confess and are saved. As the
Scripture says, "Anyone who trusts in him will never
be put to shame."*

Romans 10:9–11

Those who trust in the LORD are like Mount Zion,
    which cannot be shaken but endures forever.
As the mountains surround Jerusalem,
    so the LORD surrounds his people
    both now and forevermore.

Psalm 125:1–2

Trust in the LORD forever,
    for the LORD, the LORD, is the Rock eternal.

Isaiah 26:4

devotional thought
on trust

At least four of Jesus' disciples made their livings as fishermen. Yet as Jesus slept in the ship's bow, even these seasoned sailors panicked when the storm rose. After waking Jesus, they pleaded, "Lord, save us! We're going to drown!" (Matthew 8:25). Imagine a storm so intense that even hardened fishermen cowered in fear.

Jesus responded, "You of little faith, why are you so afraid?" (verse 26). As the disciples faced the greatest storm Galilee ever threw at them, Jesus expected them to trust him first. And then he calmed the storm.

Life often seems to rise up against us when we least expect it. A dark spot shows up on an X-ray. A quarterly report reveals a serious downturn in revenues. Suddenly, our deepest fears rise to the surface. So we look to the sky and plead, "Lord, save us!"

And Jesus says, "Don't be afraid. Trust me first."

promises for life
on unity

May the God who gives endurance and encouragement give you a spirit of unity among yourselves as you follow Christ Jesus, so that with one heart and mouth you may glorify the God and Father of our Lord Jesus Christ.

Romans 15:5–6

How good and pleasant it is
    when brothers live together in unity!

Psalm 133:1

Agree with one another so that there may be no divisions among you and that you may be perfectly united in mind and thought.

1 Corinthians 1:10

It was [Christ] who gave some to be apostles, some to be prophets, some to be evangelists, and some to be pastors and teachers, to prepare God's people for works of service, so that the body of Christ may be built up until we all reach unity in the faith.

Ephesians 4:11–13

Make every effort to keep the unity of the Spirit through the bond of peace.

Ephesians 4:3

If you have any encouragement from being united with Christ, if any comfort from his love, if any fellowship with the Spirit, if any tenderness and compassion, then make my joy complete by being like-minded, having the same love, being one in spirit and purpose.

Philippians 2:1–2

Jesus said, "By this all men will know that you are my disciples, if you love one another."

John 13:35

My purpose is that they may be encouraged in heart and united in love, so that they may have the full riches of complete understanding, in order that they may know the mystery of God, namely, Christ, in whom are hidden all the treasures of wisdom and knowledge.

Colossians 2:2–3

for men

Jesus prayed, "I pray also for those who will believe in me through their message, that all of them may be one, Father, just as you are in me and I am in you. May they also be in us so that the world may believe that you have sent me. I have given them the glory that you gave me, that they may be one as we are one: I in them and you in me. May they be brought to complete unity to let the world know that you sent me and have loved them even as you have loved me."

John 17:20–23

There before me was a great multitude that no one could count, from every nation, tribe, people and language, standing before [God's] throne.

Revelation 7:9

devotional thought
on unity

Isn't it interesting that Jesus spent some of his final hours on earth praying that his remaining followers would be known for their love for each other, and that their relationships would resemble the kind of unity he shared with his heavenly Father?

Of course, only God answers prayer. But when it comes to unity in the church, we can take some practical steps to be a part of the answer to Jesus' prayer. We can start by praying for unity in our own churches and among church leaders. We can also encourage and promote understanding when we see Christians get caught up in disagreements. Further, we can pursue love and practice self-sacrifice in our own relationships.

When the body of Christ doesn't work to build unity, the world sees a sick and weakly church. But when we join together in unity, the world sees Jesus through us.

promises for life
on wisdom

The fear of the Lord—that is wisdom,
 and to shun evil is understanding.

Job 28:28

Those who are wise will shine like the brightness of
the heavens.

Daniel 12:3

Do not be wise in your own eyes;
 fear the LORD and shun evil.
This will bring health to your body
 and nourishment to your bones.

Proverbs 3:7–8

*We have not stopped praying for you and asking God
to fill you with the knowledge of his will through all
spiritual wisdom and understanding.*

Colossians 1:9

The fear of the LORD teaches a man wisdom,
 and humility comes before honor.

Proverbs 15:33

Understanding is a fountain of life to those who
have it.

Proverbs 16:22

Choose my instruction instead of silver,
knowledge rather than choice gold,
for wisdom is more precious than rubies,
and nothing you desire can compare with her.

Proverbs 8:10–11

If any of you lacks wisdom, he should ask God, who gives generously to all without finding fault, and it will be given to him.

James 1:5

Surely you desire truth in the inner parts, [O LORD];
you teach me wisdom in the inmost place.

Psalm 51:6

Your word, [O LORD], is a lamp to my feet
and a light for my path.

Psalm 119:105

Instruct a wise man and he will be wiser still;
teach a righteous man and he will add to
his learning.

Proverbs 9:9

A man of understanding delights in wisdom.

Proverbs 10:23

promises for life
on wisdom

He who gets wisdom loves his own soul;
    he who cherishes understanding prospers.

Proverbs 19:8

A wise man has great power,
    and a man of knowledge increases strength.

Proverbs 24:5

Wisdom is supreme; therefore get wisdom.
    Though it cost all you have, get understanding.
Esteem her, and she will exalt you;
    embrace her, and she will honor you.
She will set a garland of grace on your head
    and present you with a crown of splendor.

Proverbs 4:7–9

Pride only breeds quarrels,
    but wisdom is found in those who take advice.

Proverbs 13:10

A man of understanding keeps a straight course.

Proverbs 15:21

The foolishness of God is wiser than man's wisdom.

1 Corinthians 1:25

Say to wisdom, "You are my sister,"
  and call understanding your kinsman.

Proverbs 7:4

Blessed is the man who finds wisdom,
  the man who gains understanding,
for she is more profitable than silver
  and yields better returns than gold.

Proverbs 3:13 – 14

*The wisdom that comes from heaven is first of all
pure; then peace-loving, considerate, submissive, full
of mercy and good fruit, impartial and sincere.*

James 3:17

Teach us to number our days aright, [O LORD,]
  that we may gain a heart of wisdom.

Psalm 90:12

By wisdom a house is built,
  and through understanding it is established;
through knowledge its rooms are filled
  with rare and beautiful treasures.

Proverbs 24:3 – 4

for men

[God's] divine power has given us everything we need for life and godliness through our knowledge of him who called us by his own glory and goodness.

2 Peter 1:3

My son, if you accept my words
and store up my commands within you,
turning your ear to wisdom
and applying your heart to understanding,
and if you call out for insight
and cry aloud for understanding,
and if you look for it as for silver
and search for it as for hidden treasure,
then you will understand the fear of the LORD
and find the knowledge of God.
For the LORD gives wisdom,
and from his mouth come knowledge and
understanding.

Proverbs 2:1–6

Grow in the grace and knowledge of our Lord and Savior Jesus Christ.

2 Peter 3:18

devotional thought
on wisdom

God appeared to Solomon in a dream, saying that Solomon could ask for whatever he wanted.

You name it. Solomon could've had it.

What did he choose? He asked for a discerning heart. A hearing heart. An attentive, obedient, and responsive heart. Solomon wanted to be able to listen to the truth and apply it. He asked God to make him wise, because wisdom understands what is true and right.

But Solomon didn't let it sit there. He nurtured and cultivated his gift. He added to his wisdom until he became legendary. Solomon's wisdom was known throughout the ancient world, and his writings pepper the pages of Scripture.

God has given each of us a measure of wisdom as well. But we also have at our disposal access to the fountainhead of all wisdom—God himself. His words are recorded in his book, where the pursuit of wisdom really begins.

on work

Do you see a man skilled in his work?
> He will serve before kings.

Proverbs 22:29

Obey your earthly masters with respect and fear, and with sincerity of heart, just as you would obey Christ. Obey them not only to win their favor when their eye is on you, but like slaves of Christ, doing the will of God from your heart. Serve wholeheartedly, as if you were serving the Lord, not men, because you know that the Lord will reward everyone for whatever good he does.

Ephesians 6:5–8

The desires of the diligent are fully satisfied.

Proverbs 13:4

May the favor of the Lord our God rest upon us;
> establish the work of our hands for us—
> yes, establish the work of our hands.

Psalm 90:17

Diligent hands will rule.

Proverbs 12:24

Those who have believing masters are not to show less respect for them because they are brothers. Instead, they are to serve them even better, because those who benefit from their service are believers, and dear to them.

1 Timothy 6:2

Whether you eat or drink or whatever you do, do it all for the glory of God.

1 Corinthians 10:31

Always give yourselves fully to the work of the Lord, because you know that your labor in the Lord is not in vain.

1 Corinthians 15:58

for men

Diligent hands bring wealth.

Proverbs 10:4

God is not unjust; he will not forget your work and the love you have shown him as you have helped his people and continue to help them. We want each of you to show this same diligence to the very end, in order to make your hope sure. We do not want you to become lazy, but to imitate those who through faith and patience inherit what has been promised.

Hebrews 6:10–12

Jesus said, "Behold, I am coming soon! My reward is with me, and I will give to everyone according to what he has done."

Revelation 22:12

devotional thought
on work

God provides Daniel and his three friends as an example of how a faithful follower of God functions in the working world. Daniel stood unmatched in his wisdom and skills as the king's adviser. Yet his unwavering commitment to the integrity of his relationship with God kept him from defiling himself with the king's food and drink. Daniel's integrity came before his loyalty—he served under God first and Nebuchadnezzar second, never confusing the order.

What will you do? Daniel provides the answer. Commit yourself first to the integrity of your relationship with God, and then demonstrate your loyalty to the position to which he calls you. Don't confuse the order. And let God take care of the rest.

promises for life
on worship

Jesus said, "God is spirit, and his worshipers must worship in spirit and in truth."

John 4:24

Come, let us bow down in worship,
    let us kneel before the LORD our Maker;
for he is our God
    and we are the people of his pasture,
    the flock under his care.

Psalm 95:6–7

Ascribe to the LORD, O mighty ones,
    ascribe to the LORD glory and strength.
Ascribe to the LORD the glory due his name;
    worship the LORD in the splendor of his
        holiness.

Psalm 29:1–2

Sing joyfully to the LORD, you righteous;
    it is fitting for the upright to praise him.
Praise the LORD with the harp;
    make music to him on the ten-stringed lyre.
Sing to him a new song;
    play skillfully, and shout for joy.

Psalm 33:1–3

I will extol the LORD at all times;
    his praise will always be on my lips.
My soul will boast in the LORD;
    let the afflicted hear and rejoice.
Glorify the LORD with me;
    let us exalt his name together.

Psalm 34:1–3

Praise be to the LORD, the God of Israel,
    from everlasting to everlasting.

Psalm 41:13

I have seen you in the sanctuary
    and beheld your power and your glory.
Because your love is better than life,
    my lips will glorify you.
I will praise you as long as I live,
    and in your name I will lift up my hands.

Psalm 63:2–4

Exalt the LORD our God
    and worship at his footstool;
    he is holy.

Psalm 99:5

promises for life
on worship

God is the King of all the earth;
    sing to him a psalm of praise.
God reigns over the nations;
    God is seated on his holy throne.

Psalm 47:7–8

Great is the LORD, and most worthy of praise,
    in the city of our God, his holy mountain.
It is beautiful in its loftiness,
    the joy of the whole earth.

Psalm 48:1–2

O Lord, open my lips,
    and my mouth will declare your praise.
You do not delight in sacrifice, or I would bring it;
    you do not take pleasure in burnt offerings.
The sacrifices of God are a broken spirit;
    a broken and contrite heart,
    O God, you will not despise.

Psalm 51:15–17

I rejoiced with those who said to me,
    "Let us go to the house of the LORD."

Psalm 122:1

for men

Since we are receiving a kingdom that cannot be shaken, let us be thankful, and so worship God acceptably with reverence and awe, for our "God is a consuming fire."

Hebrews 12:28–29

I will praise you forever for what you have done,
> [O Lord];
>> in your name I will hope, for your name is good.
>> I will praise you in the presence of your saints.

Psalm 52:9

You are worthy, our Lord and God,
> *to receive glory and honor and power,*
for you created all things,
> *and by your will they were created*
> *and have their being.*

Revelation 4:11

To him who sits on the throne and to the Lamb
be praise and honor and glory and power,
> *for ever and ever!*

Revelation 5:13

promises for life
on worship

Holy, holy , holy is the LORD Almighty;
   the whole earth is full of his glory.

Isaiah 6:3

One thing I ask of the LORD,
   this is what I seek:
that I may dwell in the house of the LORD
   all the days of my life,
to gaze upon the beauty of the LORD
   and to seek him in his temple.

Psalm 27:4

God exalted him to the highest place
   and gave him the name that is above every name,
that at the name of Jesus every knee should bow,
   in heaven and on earth and under the earth,
and every tongue confess that Jesus Christ is Lord,
   to the glory of God the Father.

Philippians 2:9–11

From the rising of the sun to the place where it sets,
   the name of the LORD is to be praised.

Psalm 113:3

Worthy is the Lamb, who was slain,
to receive power and wealth and wisdom and strength
and honor and glory and praise!

Revelation 5:12

Sing to God, O kingdoms of the earth,
    sing praise to the Lord,
to him who rides the ancient skies above,
    who thunders with mighty voice.
Proclaim the power of God,
    whose majesty is over Israel,
    whose power is in the skies.
You are awesome, O God, in your sanctuary;
    the God of Israel gives power and strength to
        his people.

Psalm 68:32–35

Praise our God,
    all you his servants,
you who fear him,
    both small and great!

Revelation 19:5

Great is the LORD and most worthy of praise;
    he is to be feared above all gods.
For all the gods of the nations are idols,
    but the LORD made the heavens.
Splendor and majesty are before him;
    strength and glory are in his sanctuary.

Psalm 96:4–6

The LORD reigns, let the earth be glad;
    let the distant shores rejoice.

Psalm 97:1

Hallelujah!
    For our Lord God Almighty reigns.
Let us rejoice and be glad
    and give him glory!

Revelation 19:6–7

Praise and glory
and wisdom and thanks and honor
and power and strength
be to our God for ever and ever.
Amen!

Revelation 7:12

devotional thought
on worship

When we worship, we go on a journey. Worship leads us to encounter and experience the living God. As worshippers, we do our best to prepare ourselves—purifying our hearts, clearing our minds, opening our ears, keeping our promises, and humbling our posture before God.

What are a few tactics to prepare oneself for worship? Praying for focus during the service. Listening attentively to the words being sung. Reading the Bible passages to be examined.

Focus on the fact that "God is in heaven, and you are on earth" (Ecclesiastes 5:2), understanding that you're entering the very presence of a holy and awesome God who listens, watches, and loves to hear our worship. A heart that's properly prepared for worship doesn't simply endure the journey. It prepares itself for a marvelous adventure into the presence of the God of the universe. And it expects and works toward a deeper relationship with the Creator.

We want to hear from you. Please send your comments about this book to us in care of zreview@zondervan.com. Thank you.